RISOTTO

KATHRYN HAWKINS AND JENNY STACEY

RISOTTO

OVER 120 HEALTHY AND DELICIOUS "**LITTLE RICE**" RECIPES

APPLE

A QUINTET BOOK

Published by the Apple Press
6 Blundell Street, London N7 9BH

ISBN 1-84092-252-4

This book was designed and produced by
Quintet Publishing Limited, 6 Blundell Street, London N7 9BH

Creative Director: Richard Dewing
Art Director: Simon Daley
Senior Project Editor: Laura Price
Designer: Rod Teasdale
Editor: Pamela Ellis
Photographer: Paola Zucchi
Food Stylists: Julz Beresford and Kathryn Hawkins

Typeset in Great Britain by Central Southern Typesetters, Eastbourne
Manufactured in Hong Kong by Regent Publishing Services Ltd.
Printed in China by Leefung-Asco Printers Ltd.

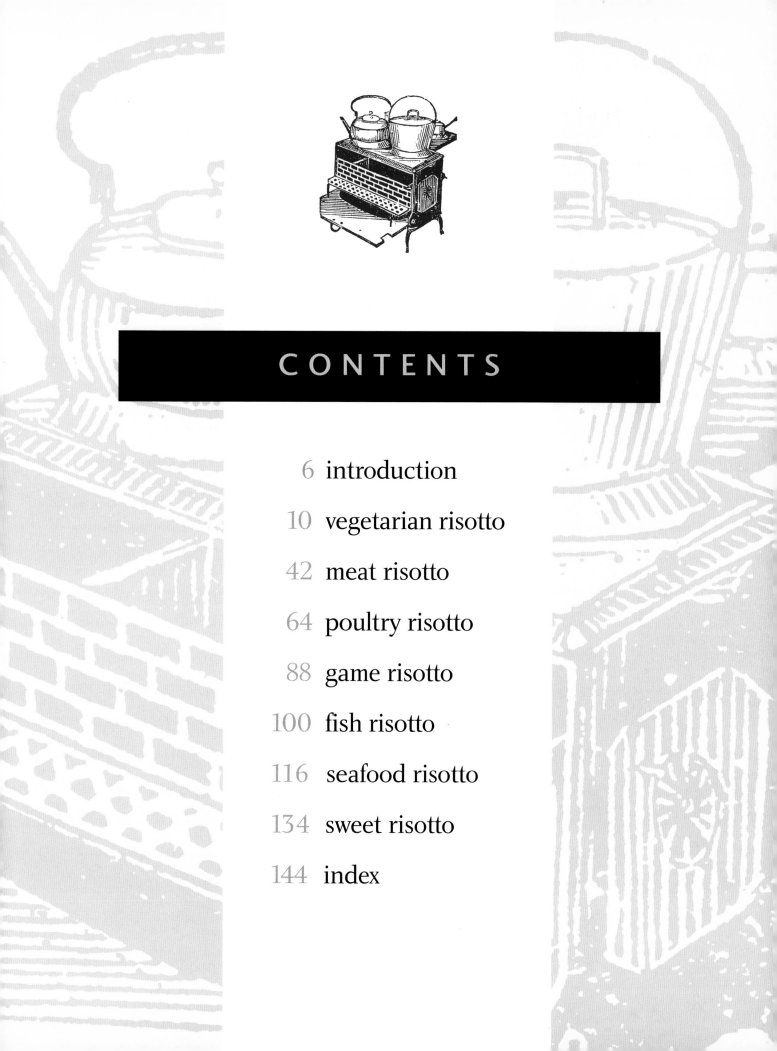

CONTENTS

ALL ABOUT RISOTTO

"RISOTTO" MEANS "**LITTLE RICE**". IT IS AN ITALIAN DISH THAT CAN BE FLAVOURED WITH MEAT, POULTRY, FISH, VEGETABLES, SHELLFISH AND GAME, AND SERVED AS A MAIN COURSE OR STARTER.

Risotto is cooked in a large wide pan in stock, or a mixture of stock and wine, and flavoured with the ingredients described. It may also be simply flavoured with cheese or saffron and served as a side dish. The most famous example is *risotto alla Milanese* which is traditionally served with *Osso Buco*. Whether risotto is served as the starter, main course, or even dessert, the remainder of the meal should be light.

Rice, the basis of risotto, is nutritious as well as delicious. Being a complex carbohydrate, it contains starch and fibre and is digested slowly. It is also a good source of potassium and the B vitamins niacin and thiamin. A 50-gram (2-ounce) raw portion of rice also provides approximately 10% of an adult's R.D.A. of protein. Containing virtually no cholesterol or fat, rice is ideal for those watching their fat intake. It is also gluten-free, making it suitable for people who suffer from coeliac disease. Additional ingredients may increase fat and calorie counts, however, so it should not always be considered healthy, especially if cream or high-fat meat is added.

Risottos are one of the most delicious yet simple Italian dishes. The technique of cooking short-grain rice is traditional and involves stirring hot stock gradually into the rice. A variety of ingredients are added to the basic risotto recipe to produce many combinations of colour, flavour, and texture. Because rice is so filling, a risotto makes an economical meal for a family, its versatility never allowing for boredom. Risottos are best eaten freshly cooked, but some may be frozen if their flavourings allow. In this case, do not completely cook the rice, cool it, then freeze. Defrost the risotto thoroughly and reheat with additional butter or oil until completely hot right through and creamy in texture.

In the Veneto region of Italy, the dish is so popular it commands its own festival. The four-day celebration enables guests to taste a host of risotto recipes, and competition for the best recipe is fierce. Risotto is cooked on the streets in huge iron pans, and guests are invited to indulge at their will.

some essentials

To achieve the characteristic creamy consistency of risotto, there are a few points to consider. The first and most important of these is the type of rice used.

THE RICE The high starch quantity of these grains allows them to absorb liquid slowly, resulting in a creamy texture without a loss of bite. It is therefore important that the rice is not washed before cooking or some of the starch will be removed and the texture of the finished dish will be more grainy. Long-grain rice will not give the desired result. To achieve the required texture, only authentic risotto rice should be used for these recipes. This is not a problem as the most common one, arborio rice, is widely available. There are three risotto rices that are all grown in Italy. The first of these is *Vialone nano*, a medium-grain, round rice which is grown in the Veneto. It has a less creamy texture than the following varieties. *Arborio* rice is a plump,

longer-grained rice from Piedmont. It will absorb a high quantity of liquid without losing its *al dente* bite, and is classed as a "superfino" rice. It gives a delicious, creamy result. The final rice, *carnaroli*, is a smaller superfino-grain rice than arborio and is from the Lombardy region. It too will absorb large quantities of liquid without becoming soggy.

THE STOCK The second point to consider when making risotto is the stock. If possible, use a good home-made stock, varying the flavour according to the recipe. Use fish, beef, chicken, lamb, vegetable or pork stock. If this is not possible, aim to use a good-quality prepared stock. This will add fantastic flavour to the dish as the rice absorbs it while cooking.

THE PAN Thirdly, choose your pan carefully. A wide heavy-based pan is best. It should be quite deep, to help to slow the evaporation of the liquid, but not so deep that it is difficult to stir the risotto thoroughly.

cooking risotto

The correct heat should be maintained during cooking. If the dish is cooked on too high a heat, the liquid will evaporate too quickly for the rice to absorb it. If too low a heat is used, slow cooking will give a soggy result and the rice will not cook evenly. A perfect risotto is neither too runny nor too dry, but tender and creamy, with the grains holding together, yet separate.

The actual cooking method is simple, but requires constant attention. Here are a few tips to consider for the perfect risotto.

Firstly, heat the stock, or stock and wine, if using a mixture, to boiling point. Reduce the heat to maintain a gentle simmer throughout the cooking time. Adding hot liquid makes the rice grains swell, but keeps them firm. It also ensures the continuous cooking of the rice. If cold liquid is added the rice will take longer to cook and the required texture will not be obtained.

When you begin to prepare your risotto and fry your onion it is important not to let the onion brown because the dish will be too sweet and the colour will be wrong.

When the rice is coated in the butter and oil mixture, add a small quantity of hot stock to the rice and stir it in until it is completely absorbed. After this, continue to add the hot stock in small quantities, allowing for absorption in between. Constant stirring ensures that the rice evenly absorbs the liquid and maintains an even consistency while cooking.

Do not try to rush the cooking process by turning up the heat or adding the stock more quickly. This will simply ruin the final dish.

The liquid quantities and timings of the recipes given in this book are approximate. Some dishes may require more or less liquid and a longer or shorter cooking time, depending on the heat, the pan used, the type of rice, and the other ingredients.

serving risotto

Ideally, the risotto should rest for a few minutes before serving in warm, shallow bowls or plates. It is often served with freshly grated Parmesan, topped with fresh herbs and accompanied by a glass of Italian wine.

The recipes here demonstrate the versatility of this delicious dish, covering a range of dishes using vegetables, meat, poultry, fish and shellfish, and game. Each recipe serves 4 as a main course or 6 to 8 as a starter or side dish.

There are even some sweet fruit and chocolate recipes, that will make a perfect finale to a meal, each serving 4 as dessert.

making the perfect basic risotto

1 Heat the stock then cook onion, garlic and other flavourings in butter or butter and oil, in a large shallow pan. Stir in the unwashed rice and cook, stirring constantly, for 2 minutes. Keep the rice moving in the pan until it is well coated in the butter and oil. This will ensure the rice cooks evenly and is well flavoured.

2 The stock should be added in small quantities. Allowing the rice to absorb the liquid between each addition is vital for the creamy texture that is characteristic of risotto. Once the stock has been added, if the risotto becomes too dry, add hot water. It should take approximately 20 minutes for the dish to cook after this initial addition of stock.

3 The risotto is ready to eat when a creamy texture has been achieved. The rice should be firm to the bite, but tender. It should be neither chalky nor soggy. Add butter or any further ingredients, garnish and serve.

4 Some risottos benefit from *mantecare* – being covered and left to rest for several minutes when ready, with extra butter or cheese, or both, stirred in. This makes the texture even more creamy.

VEGETARIAN RISOTTO

Mediterranean Vegetable Risotto

Risotto Verde

Risotto Rosso

Risotto Giallo

Risotto Bianco

Asparagus Risotto

Green Vegetable Risotto

Olive and Caper Tomato Risotto

Olive Risotto

Risotto with Squash

Blue Cheese Pumpkin Risotto

Risotto alla Milanese

Orange Fennel Risotto

Lemon Shallot Risotto

Orange Sage and Mushroom Risotto

Buttery Pumpkin and Hazelnut Risotto

Mixed Onion Risotto

Spinach and Raisin Risotto

Four-cheese Risotto

Spinach and Gorgonzola Risotto

Saffron, Pepper and Marsala Risotto

Red Onion Tomato Risotto

Mixed Vegetable and Bean Risotto

Pilaf-style Risotto

Risotto con Vermicelli

Chilli Bean Risotto

Oriental Vegetable Risotto

mediterranean
vegetable risotto

THIS RISOTTO MAKES A STUNNING MAIN COURSE. FOR A SIMPLE MEAL, SERVE WITH HERB OR CHEESE BREAD.

1 medium aubergine

2 medium courgettes

1 red pepper

2 medium tomatoes

1 red onion

2 cloves garlic

6 Tbsp olive oil

**2 Tbsp chopped fresh rosemary or
   2 tsp dried**

1.25 l (2 pts) vegetable stock

1 medium onion, finely chopped

400 g (14 oz) arborio rice

150 ml (¼ pt) dry white wine

Salt and freshly ground black pepper

**50 g (2 oz) diced or crumbled feta
   cheese**

Fresh rosemary, to garnish

1 First prepare the vegetables. Trim and dice the aubergine into 2.5-cm (1-in) pieces. Trim and slice the courgettes. Seed and dice the pepper into 2.5-cm (1-in) cubes. Quarter the tomatoes. Peel and cut the red onion into eight wedges. Peel and thinly slice the garlic.

2 Place all the vegetables in a bowl and gently stir in five tablespoons olive oil and the rosemary until well mixed. Preheat the grill. Grill the vegetables for 8 to 10 minutes, turning frequently, until lightly charred and tender. Set aside.

3 Pour the stock into a saucepan and bring to the boil. Reduce the heat to a gentle simmer.

4 Meanwhile, heat the remaining oil in a large saucepan and gently fry the onion for 2 to 3 minutes until softened. Add the rice and cook, stirring, for 2 minutes until well-coated in the onion mixture.

5 Add the wine and cook gently, stirring, until absorbed. Ladle in the stock gradually, until all the liquid is absorbed and the rice is thick, creamy and tender. Keep the heat moderate. This will take about 25 minutes. Season well.

6 Gently stir in the prepared vegetables and heat through for 2 to 3 minutes until hot. Serve sprinkled with the cheese and garnished with fresh rosemary.

risotto verde

THIS FRESH-TASTING DISH IS THE PERFECT
ACCOMPANIMENT TO FISH AND POULTRY DISHES.

1.25 l (2 pts) vegetable
stock

2 Tbsp vegetable oil

1 large onion, finely
chopped

2 green peppers, seeded
and chopped

400 g (14 oz) arborio rice

150 ml (¼ pt) dry white
wine

225 g (8 oz) frozen or
freshly shelled peas

2 tsp ground coriander

Salt and freshly ground
black pepper

4 Tbsp chopped fresh
coriander

2 spring onions, finely
chopped

1 Pour the stock into a saucepan and bring to the boil.
Reduce the heat to a gentle simmer.

2 Meanwhile, heat the oil in a large saucepan and
gently fry the onion and peppers for 3 to
4 minutes until just softened but not browned. Add the
rice and cook, stirring, for 2 minutes until well-coated in
the pepper mixture.

3 Add the wine and cook gently, stirring, until
absorbed. Ladle in the stock gradually, until half the
liquid is absorbed. Mix in the peas. Continue ladling in
the stock until the rice is thick, creamy and tender. The
heat should be moderate. This will take about 25 minutes.

4 Stir in the ground coriander and seasoning. Then
mix in the fresh coriander and serve sprinkled with
the finely chopped spring onions.

risotto rosso

THE VIBRANT COLOUR OF THIS DISH COMES FROM THE
FRESH BEETROOT. SPOON OVER SOURED CREAM TO SERVE
AND ACCOMPANY WITH CRUSTY BREAD AND FRESHLY
STEAMED GREEN VEGETABLES.

1.25 l (2 pts) vegetable
stock

2 Tbsp butter

1 Tbsp olive oil

2 medium red onions,
thinly sliced

4 medium fresh raw
beetroots, peeled
and finely sliced or
coarsely grated

2 carrots, coarsely grated

400 g (14 oz) arborio rice

150 ml (¼ pt) red wine

Salt and freshly ground
black pepper

4 Tbsp soured cream

Snipped fresh chives, to
garnish

1 Pour the stock into a saucepan and bring to the boil.
Reduce the heat to a gentle simmer.

2 Meanwhile, melt the butter with the oil in a large
saucepan and gently fry the onions, beetroot and
carrot for 10 minutes until just beginning to soften. Add
the rice and cook, stirring, for 2 minutes until well-coated
in the vegetable mixture.

3 Add the red wine and cook gently, stirring, until
absorbed. Ladle in the stock gradually over moderate
heat until all the liquid is absorbed and the rice is thick,
creamy and tender. This will take about 25 minutes.

4 Add seasoning to taste. Serve immediately, topped
with soured cream and sprinkled with chives.

OPPOSITE **RISOTTO ROSSO**

risotto giallo

THE SUNNY COLOURS IN THIS DISH WILL BRIGHTEN UP ANY MEAL. FOR MAXIMUM IMPACT, SERVE THE RISOTTO WITH CONTRASTING COLOURED SALADS.

1.25 l (2 pts) vegetable stock

2 Tbsp butter

1 Tbsp vegetable oil

1 large onion, finely chopped

1 yellow pepper, seeded and chopped

225 g (8 oz) pumpkin or yellow squash flesh, diced

400 g (14 oz) arborio rice

Large pinch saffron

Salt and white pepper

350-g (12-oz) tin corn, drained

Halved grilled yellow tomatoes, to garnish

1 Pour the stock into a saucepan and bring to the boil. Reduce the heat to a gentle simmer.

2 Meanwhile, melt the butter with the oil in a large saucepan and gently fry the onion, pepper and pumpkin for 4 to 5 minutes until just softened. Add the rice and cook, stirring, for 2 minutes until the rice is well-coated in the vegetable mixture.

3 Add a ladleful of stock and cook gently, stirring until absorbed. Continue ladling in the stock until half of it is used. Sprinkle in the saffron and seasoning. Mix in the corn.

4 Continue adding the stock until all the liquid is absorbed and the rice is thick, creamy and tender. Keep the heat moderate. This will take about 25 minutes. Garnish with the tomatoes and serve.

risotto bianco

THIS RISOTTO IS A SIMPLE COMBINATION OF MUSHROOMS AND RICE WITH JUST A HINT OF THYME AND CREAM.

1.25 l (2 pts) vegetable stock

50 g (2 oz) garlic and herb butter

1 medium onion, finely chopped

1 clove garlic, crushed

225 g (8 oz) sliced button mushrooms

1 tsp dried or 4 tsp fresh thyme

400 g (14 oz) arborio rice

Salt and white pepper

4 Tbsp extra-dry vermouth

4 Tbsp double cream

Fresh thyme, to garnish

1 Pour the stock into a saucepan and bring to the boil. Reduce the heat to a gentle simmer.

2 Meanwhile, melt the butter and gently fry the onion, garlic, mushrooms and thyme for 3 to 4 minutes until softened but not browned. Add the rice and cook, stirring, for 2 minutes until well-coated in the mushroom mixture. Season.

3 Add a ladleful of stock and cook gently, stirring, until absorbed. Continue adding the stock, ladle by ladle, until all the liquid is absorbed and the rice is thick, creamy and tender. Keep the heat moderate. This will take about 25 minutes. Stir in the vermouth and cream. Garnish and serve.

OPPOSITE RISOTTO BIANCO

asparagus risotto

LIGHTLY COOKED ASPARAGUS IS ADDED TO THIS SIMPLE RISOTTO. IT CAN BE SERVED ON ITS OWN AS A SUBSTANTIAL STARTER, SIDE DISH OR SUPPER.

225 g (8 oz) asparagus spears

1.25 l (2 pts) vegetable stock (see method)

1 Tbsp olive oil

1 medium onion, finely chopped

400 g (14 oz) arborio rice

4 Tbsp extra-dry vermouth

4 Tbsp double cream

Salt and freshly ground black pepper

25 g (1 oz) freshly grated Parmesan cheese (optional)

1 Cut off the very woody ends from the asparagus. Cut the spears into 5-cm (2-in) lengths. Bring a small saucepan of water to the boil and cook the asparagus for 4 to 5 minutes until just cooked. Drain and set aside. Reserve the cooking liquid and use to make up the stock.

2 Pour the stock into a saucepan and bring to the boil. Reduce the heat to a gentle simmer.

3 Meanwhile, heat the oil in a large saucepan and gently fry the onion for 2 to 3 minutes until softened but not browned. Add the rice and cook, stirring, for 2 minutes.

4 Add a ladleful of stock and cook gently, stirring, until absorbed. Continue ladling in the stock until all the liquid has been absorbed and the rice is thick, creamy and tender. Keep the heat moderate. This will take about 25 minutes.

5 Stir in the vermouth and cream. Gently mix in the cooked asparagus and season. Serve sprinkled with Parmesan, if using.

green vegetable risotto

MAKES AN EXCELLENT ACCOMPANIMENT TO MEAT OR FISH, AND CAN ALSO BE SERVED AS A VEGETARIAN MAIN COURSE.

225 g (8 oz) small broccoli florets

125 g (4 oz) fine asparagus spears

225 g (8 oz) Savoy cabbage, shredded

1.25 l (2 pts) vegetable stock (see method)

50 g (2 oz) garlic and herb butter

4 trimmed and shredded small leeks

400 g (14 oz) arborio rice

Salt and freshly ground black pepper

4 Tbsp chopped fresh parsley

1 Bring a saucepan of water to the boil and cook the broccoli for 3 to 4 minutes until just tender; cook the asparagus and cabbage for 1 minute until just tender. Reserving the cooking water, drain the vegetables and set aside. Use the water to make up the stock.

2 Pour the stock into a saucepan and bring to the boil. Reduce the heat to a gentle simmer.

3 Meanwhile, melt the garlic and herb butter in a large saucepan and gently fry the leeks for 2 to 3 minutes until softened but not browned. Stir in the rice and cook, stirring, for 2 minutes until the rice is well-coated.

4 Add a ladleful of stock and cook gently over moderate heat, stirring, until absorbed. Season well. Continue adding the stock, ladle by ladle, until the risotto is thick, but not sticky, and the rice is tender. This will take about 25 minutes.

5 Stir in the cooked vegetables and chopped parsley, and heat through for 2 to 3 minutes until hot. Serve immediately.

OPPOSITE **ASPARAGUS RISOTTO**

olive & caper tomato risotto

THE TRADITIONAL COMBINATION OF INGREDIENTS IN THIS RISOTTO GIVES IT A THOROUGHLY ITALIAN FLAVOUR.

950 ml (1½ pts) vegetable stock

2 Tbsp olive oil

1 large onion, finely chopped

1 clove garlic, minced

400 g (14 oz) arborio rice

1 tsp dried or 4 tsp fresh mixed herbs

150 ml (¼ pt) red wine

400 g (14 oz) tin chopped tomatoes

Salt and freshly ground black pepper

150 g (5 oz) black olives

2 Tbsp capers

Romano cheese shavings, to garnish

1 Pour the stock into a saucepan and bring to the boil. Reduce the heat to a gentle simmer.

2 Meanwhile, heat the oil in a large saucepan and gently fry the onion and garlic for 2 to 3 minutes until softened but not browned. Add the rice and herbs and cook, stirring, for 2 minutes until well-coated in the onion mixture.

3 Add the wine and chopped tomatoes and cook gently, stirring, until absorbed. Ladle in the stock gradually and cook until all the liquid is absorbed and the rice is thick, creamy and tender. This should take about 25 minutes.

4 Season well and stir in the olives and capers. Serve topped with shavings of Romano cheese and sprinkled with black pepper.

olive risotto

A MOUTHWATERING COMBINATION OF RICE AND OLIVES MAKES THIS RISOTTO AN UNUSUAL SIDE DISH, OR, FOR AN OLIVE LOVER, THE PERFECT SUPPER.

1.25 l (2 pts) vegetable stock

3 Tbsp extra-virgin olive oil

225 g (8 oz) shallots, finely sliced

2 cloves garlic, minced

400 g (14 oz) arborio rice

75 g (3 oz) stoned green olives

75 g (3 oz) pimento-stuffed green olives

75 g (3 oz) stoned black olives

Salt and freshly ground black pepper

2 Tbsp shredded basil leaves

1 Pour the stock into a saucepan and bring to the boil. Reduce the heat to a gentle simmer.

2 Meanwhile, heat two tablespoons oil in a large frying pan and gently fry the shallots and garlic for 2 to 3 minutes until softened but not browned. Add the rice and cook, stirring, for 2 minutes until well-coated in the shallot mixture.

3 Add a ladleful of stock and cook gently, stirring, until absorbed. Continue adding the stock, ladle by ladle, into the rice until all the liquid has been absorbed and the rice is thick, creamy and tender.

4 Stir in the olives and adjust the seasoning. Serve the risotto sprinkled with the basil and drizzled with the remaining oil.

OPPOSITE **OLIVE RISOTTO**

risotto with squash

SQUASH COMBINES WITH TOMATOES IN THIS
BUTTERY RISOTTO. SERVE THIS AS AN UNUSUAL
ACCOMPANIMENT TO A CASSEROLE, OR AS A
DELICIOUS MAIN MEAL.

950 ml (1 ½ pts) vegetable
stock

75 g (3 oz) butter

2 medium red onions,
finely chopped

2 cloves garlic, crushed

450 g (1 lb) butternut
squash flesh, diced

400 g (14 oz) arborio rice

Salt and freshly ground
black pepper

150 ml (¼ pt) dry white
wine

400 g (14 oz) tin chopped
tomatoes

2 Tbsp chopped fresh
parsley

1 Pour the stock into a saucepan and bring to the boil.
Reduce the heat to a gentle simmer.

2 Meanwhile, melt the butter and gently fry the onion,
garlic and squash for 7 to 8 minutes until just
softening. Add the rice and cook, stirring, for 2 minutes
until well-mixed. Season well.

3 Add the wine and chopped tomatoes and cook
gently, stirring, until absorbed. Add the stock, ladle
by ladle, until the liquid is absorbed and the rice is thick,
creamy and tender. Keep the heat moderate. This will take
about 25 minutes.

4 Adjust the seasoning if necessary. Serve sprinkled
with chopped parsley.

blue cheese pumpkin risotto

PUMPKIN HAS AN EARTHY TASTE AND ABSORBS THE
FLAVOURS FROM OTHER INGREDIENTS DURING COOKING.
IN THIS RISOTTO, IT COMBINES WITH BLUE CHEESE TO
MAKE A VERY RICH AND SURPRISINGLY DELICIOUS DISH.

1.25 l (2 pts) vegetable
stock

50 g (2 oz) butter

1 medium onion, finely
chopped

450 g (1 lb) pumpkin or
squash flesh, diced

400 g (14 oz) arborio rice

Salt and freshly ground
black pepper

50 g (2 oz) crumbled blue
cheese, such as
Gorgonzola, Stilton or
Danish blue

2 Tbsp chopped fresh
parsley

1 Pour the stock into a saucepan and bring to the boil.
Reduce the heat to a gentle simmer.

2 Meanwhile, melt the butter in a large saucepan and
gently fry the onion for 2 to 3 minutes until softened
but not browned. Add the pumpkin and continue to cook,
stirring, for 6 to 7 minutes until just beginning to soften.

3 Stir in the rice and cook, stirring, for 2 minutes until
the rice is well-coated in the pumpkin mixture. Add
the stock, ladle by ladle, until all the liquid is absorbed
and the rice is thick, creamy and tender. Keep the heat
moderate. This will take about 25 minutes.

4 Season well and gently stir in the blue cheese. Serve
sprinkled with chopped parsley.

OPPOSITE BLUE CHEESE PUMPKIN RISOTTO

risotto alla milanese

RISOTTO ALLA MILANESE IS AN ITALIAN CLASSIC. GOLDEN YELLOW IN COLOUR AND AROMATIC IN FLAVOUR, THIS DISH CAN BE SERVED AS AN ACCOMPANIMENT OR AS A SUPPER WITH CRUSTY BREAD AND SALAD.

1.25 l (2 pts) vegetable stock

75 g (3 oz) butter

1 medium onion, finely chopped

1 clove garlic, crushed

400 g (14 oz) arborio rice

Large pinch saffron

Salt and white pepper

50 g (2 oz) freshly grated Parmesan cheese

1 Pour the stock into a saucepan and bring to the boil. Reduce the heat to a gentle simmer.

2 Meanwhile, melt 50 g (2 oz) butter in a large saucepan and gently fry the onion and garlic for 2 to 3 minutes until softened but not browned. Stir in the rice and cook, stirring, for 2 minutes, until well-coated in butter.

3 Add a ladleful of stock and cook gently, stirring, until absorbed. Continue adding the stock ladle by ladle to the rice until half the stock is used and the rice is creamy. Sprinkle in the saffron and seasoning.

4 Add the remaining stock until the risotto becomes thick, but not sticky. This will take about 25 minutes and should not be hurried. Just before serving, carefully stir in the remaining butter and the Parmesan cheese. Serve immediately.

cheese & sun-dried tomato risotto

THIS IS AN EXTRA-RICH RISOTTO WITH THE DELICIOUS INTENSE TASTE OF SUN-DRIED TOMATOES, THAT CAN BE SERVED AS A SIDE DISH OR AS A SIMPLE SUPPER.

50 g (2 oz) sun-dried tomatoes, soaked as directed

1.25 l (2 pts) vegetable stock

50 g (2 oz) butter

1 medium onion, finely chopped

400 g (14 oz) arborio rice

1 tsp dried or 4 tsp fresh mixed herbs

Salt and freshly ground black pepper

75 g (3 oz) freshly grated Romano cheese

One 25-g (1-oz) piece Romano cheese

Flat leaf parsley, to garnish

1 Reserving the liquid, drain the tomatoes and slice into thin strips. Set aside.

2 Pour the stock into a saucepan and bring to the boil. Reduce the heat to a gentle simmer.

3 Meanwhile, melt the butter in a large saucepan and gently fry the onion and tomato for 2 to 3 minutes until softened but not browned. Stir in the rice and cook, stirring, for 2 minutes, until the rice is well-coated.

4 Add the tomato soaking liquid and cook gently, stirring until absorbed. Add the herbs and seasoning. Ladle in the stock, one ladleful at a time, until the liquid is absorbed and the rice is thick, creamy and tender. This will take about 25 minutes.

5 Gently stir in the grated cheese and transfer to a warmed serving dish. Garnish with parsley and shaved cheese to serve.

OPPOSITE RISOTTO ALLA MILANESE

orange fennel risotto

THIS IS A LIGHT AND FRAGRANT RISOTTO, PERFECT AS A STARTER OR SUPPER DISH.

1.25 l (2 pts) vegetable stock

2 bulbs fennel

2 Tbsp butter

1 Tbsp olive oil

2 sticks celery, trimmed and chopped

2 medium leeks, trimmed and shredded

400 g (14 oz) arborio rice

3 medium oranges

Salt and freshly ground black pepper

1 Pour the stock into a saucepan and bring to the boil. Reduce the heat to a gentle simmer.

2 Meanwhile, trim the fennel, reserving the fronds, and cut into thin slices. Melt the butter with the oil in a large saucepan and gently fry the fennel, celery and leeks for 3 to 4 minutes until just softened. Add the rice and cook, stirring, for 2 minutes until well-mixed.

3 Add a ladleful of stock and cook gently, stirring, until absorbed. Continue adding the stock, ladle by ladle, until it is all absorbed and the rice becomes creamy, thick and tender. This will take about 25 minutes and should not be hurried.

4 Remove the zest and extract the juice from 1 orange, and mix into the rice. Carefully slice off the peel and pith from the remaining oranges and, holding the fruit over the saucepan, slice out the orange sections and add to the rice, along with any juice that falls. Gently mix into the rice, season well and serve garnished with the reserved fennel fronds.

lemon shallot risotto

IN THIS DISH GOLDEN SHALLOTS ARE MIXED WITH THE DELICATE FLAVOURS OF LEMON AND FRESH TARRAGON. THIS IS THE PERFECT RISOTTO WITH FISH OR SEAFOOD.

1.25 l (2 pts) vegetable stock

1 Tbsp olive oil

2 Tbsp butter

250 g (8 oz) shallots, halved

1 Tbsp lemon juice

1 tsp sugar

400 g (14 oz) arborio rice

Finely grated zest of 1 lemon

Salt and freshly ground black pepper

2 Tbsp chopped fresh tarragon

4 Tbsp double cream

25 g (1 oz) freshly grated Parmesan cheese

Fresh tarragon and lemon zest, to garnish

1 Pour the stock into a saucepan and bring to the boil. Reduce the heat to a gentle simmer.

2 Meanwhile, heat the oil and butter in a large saucepan and fry the shallots with the lemon juice and sugar for 6 to 7 minutes until golden brown and lightly caramelized. Add the rice and cook, stirring, for 2 minutes until well-mixed.

3 Add a ladleful of stock and cook gently, stirring, until absorbed. Continue adding the stock, ladle by ladle, into the rice until half the stock is used and the rice is creamy. Sprinkle in the lemon zest and seasoning.

4 Continue adding the stock until the risotto becomes thick and the rice is tender. This will take about 25 minutes and should not be hurried. Stir in the chopped tarragon, cream and grated Parmesan cheese. Adjust the seasoning if necessary. Garnish and serve.

OPPOSITE **LEMON SHALLOT RISOTTO**

orange, sage & mushroom risotto

TANGY ORANGE AND THE AROMATIC FLAVOUR OF SAGE
ENLIVEN THIS MUSHROOM RISOTTO DISH.

950 ml (1 ½ pts) vegetable stock	400 g (14 oz) arborio rice
50 g (2 oz) garlic and herb butter	Salt and freshly ground black pepper
2 Tbsp olive oil	1 tsp powdered sage
1 medium onion, finely chopped	300 ml (½ pt) unsweetened orange juice
225 g (8 oz) sliced mushrooms	2 medium oranges
2 large mushrooms, sliced	1 Tbsp chopped fresh sage
	Orange zest, to garnish

1 Pour the stock into a saucepan and bring to the boil. Reduce the heat to a gentle simmer.

2 Meanwhile, melt the butter with the oil in a large saucepan and gently fry the onion and mushrooms for 3 to 4 minutes until just softened. Add the rice and cook, stirring, for 2 minutes until well-mixed. Season and add the powdered sage.

3 Add the orange juice and cook gently, stirring, until absorbed. Add the stock, ladle by ladle, until it is all absorbed and the rice is thick, creamy and tender. Keep the heat moderate. This will take about 25 minutes.

4 Carefully peel the oranges, removing the pith at the same time. Holding the oranges over the risotto, slice out the orange sections and gently mix them into the rice. Adjust the seasoning and mix in the chopped sage. Serve garnished with orange zest.

buttery pumpkin & hazelnut risotto

THIS DELICIOUS COMBINATION OF JUICY PUMPKIN,
NUTS AND TANGY ORANGE MAKES A MEMORABLE MAIN
COURSE DISH.

1.25 l (2 pts) vegetable stock	Grated zest of ½ orange
75 g (3 oz) butter	Salt and freshly ground black pepper
1 large onion, finely chopped	25 g (1 oz) freshly grated Parmesan cheese
450 g (1 lb) pumpkin flesh, diced	65 g (2½ oz) roasted chopped hazelnuts
2 cloves garlic, crushed	Orange zest, to garnish
400 g (14 oz) arborio rice	

1 Pour the stock into a saucepan and bring to the boil. Reduce the heat to a gentle simmer.

2 Meanwhile, melt 50 g (2 oz) butter in a large saucepan and gently fry the onion, pumpkin and garlic for 7 to 8 minutes until just softened. Add the rice and cook, stirring, for 2 minutes until well mixed.

3 Add a ladleful of stock and cook gently, stirring, until absorbed. Continue adding the stock, ladle by ladle, until half is used and the rice is creamy. Add the grated orange zest and season.

4 Continue adding the stock until the risotto is thick and the rice is tender. This will take about 25 minutes. Stir in the remaining butter and grated cheese. Sprinkle with the hazelnuts and garnish with orange zest to serve.

OPPOSITE BUTTERY PUMPKIN
AND HAZLENUT RISOTTO

walnut, garlic & thyme risotto

THIS RISOTTO IS ENRICHED WITH WALNUTS AND THEIR OIL. SERVE WITH A LIGHT GREEN SALAD.

1.25 l (2 pts) vegetable stock	400 g (14 oz) arborio rice
2 Tbsp butter	Salt and freshly ground black pepper
1 Tbsp olive oil	1 Tbsp walnut oil
4 cloves garlic, crushed	65 g (2½ oz) walnut pieces
65 g (2½ oz) very finely chopped walnuts	Sprig fresh thyme, to garnish
2 Tbsp chopped fresh thyme or 2 tsp dried	

1 Pour the stock into a saucepan and bring to the boil. Reduce the heat to a gentle simmer.

2 Meanwhile, melt the butter with the oil in a large saucepan and gently fry the garlic, chopped walnuts and thyme for 2 minutes. Stir in the rice and cook, stirring, for a further 2 minutes until the rice is well-coated in the walnut mixture.

3 Add the stock, ladle by ladle, until all the liquid is absorbed and the rice is thick, creamy and tender. Keep the heat moderate. This will take about 25 minutes and should not be hurried.

4 Adjust the seasoning and stir in the walnut oil. Serve the risotto sprinkled with the walnut pieces and garnish with thyme.

fragrant herb risotto

USE ANY COMBINATION OF YOUR FAVOURITE HERBS IN THIS RECIPE. THEIR DELICATE FLAVOURS ARE ENHANCED BY THE ADDITION OF WHITE WINE, MAKING THIS THE PERFECT ACCOMPANIMENT TO A FISH MEAL.

950 ml (1½ pts) vegetable stock	Salt and freshly ground black pepper
2 Tbsp olive oil	2 Tbsp each of chopped fresh parsley, sage, basil, marjoram and tarragon
2 medium leeks, trimmed and shredded	
400 g (14 oz) arborio rice	2 Tbsp soured cream
300 ml (½ pt) dry white wine	Mixed fresh herbs, to garnish

1 Pour the stock into a saucepan and bring to the boil. Reduce the heat to a gentle simmer.

2 Meanwhile, heat the oil in a large saucepan and gently fry the leeks for 2 to 3 minutes until softened but not browned. Add the rice and cook, stirring, for 2 minutes until the rice is well-coated in the leek mixture.

3 Pour in half the wine and cook gently, stirring, until absorbed. Add the remaining wine, and ladle in the stock gradually until all the liquid is absorbed and the rice is thick, creamy and tender. Keep the heat moderate. This will take about 25 minutes.

4 Season. Stir in the chopped herbs and cream. Garnish and serve.

OPPOSITE FRAGRANT HERB RISOTTO

mixed onion risotto

THIS DISH MAKES A TASTY ACCOMPANIMENT TO ROAST
MEATS OR ROASTED VEGETABLES.

1.25 l (2 pts) vegetable
stock

50 g (2 oz) butter

1 Tbsp vegetable oil

225 g (8 oz) shallots,
halved

2 medium onions, finely
sliced

2 medium red onions,
finely chopped

1 Tbsp lemon juice

2 tsp sugar

400 g (14 oz) arborio rice

150 ml ($\frac{1}{4}$ pt) dry white
wine

Salt and freshly ground
black pepper

4 Tbsp snipped fresh
chives

1 Pour the stock into a saucepan and bring to the boil.
Reduce the heat to a gentle simmer.

2 Meanwhile, melt the butter with the oil in a large
saucepan and fry the shallots and onions with the
lemon juice and sugar for 8 to 10 minutes until richly
golden and caramelized. Stir in the rice and cook,
stirring, for a further 2 minutes until well-mixed.

3 Add the wine and cook gently, stirring, until
absorbed. Add the stock, ladle by ladle, until all the
liquid is absorbed and the rice is thick, creamy and
tender. Keep the heat moderate. This will take about
25 minutes and should not be hurried. Season well.
Stir in the chives and serve.

spinach & raisin
risotto

SPINACH AND NUTMEG IS A CLASSIC COMBINATION
THAT IS IDEAL SERVED AS AN ACCOMPANIMENT TO A
RICH MEAT CASSEROLE.

1 kg (2 lb) young spinach
leaves, trimmed

1.25 l (2 pts) vegetable
stock

50 g (2 oz) butter

1 medium onion, finely
chopped

400 g (14 oz) arborio rice

1 tsp freshly grated
nutmeg

50 g (2 oz) seedless raisins

50 g (2 oz) toasted pine
kernels

Salt and freshly ground
black pepper

1 Wash the spinach leaves and place in a large pan
while they are still wet. Cover and set over high heat
for 4 to 5 minutes until wilted. There will be sufficient
water on the spinach from washing to steam the leaves.
Reserving any cooking liquid, drain the spinach well and
roughly chop. Set aside.

2 Pour the stock into a saucepan and bring to the boil.
Reduce the heat to a gentle simmer.

3 Meanwhile, melt the butter in a large saucepan
and gently fry the onion for 2 to 3 minutes until
softened but not browned. Stir in the rice and cook,
stirring, for 2 minutes until the rice is well-coated in
the onion mixture.

4 Add the spinach cooking water to the rice and cook
gently, stirring, until absorbed. Add the stock, ladle
by ladle, until the liquid is absorbed and the rice thickens
and is creamy and tender. Keep the heat moderate. This
will take about 25 minutes.

5 Mix in the nutmeg, cooked spinach, raisins and pine
kernels. Season well and serve.

OPPOSITE **SPINACH AND RAISIN RISOTTO**

four-cheese risotto

THIS DISH USES A RICH COMBINATION OF CREAMY
CHEESES. SERVE AS A MAIN MEAL WITH FRESHLY
STEAMED VEGETABLES.

1.25 l (2 pts) vegetable stock	25 g (1 oz) freshly grated Parmesan cheese
50 g (2 oz) butter	50 g (2 oz) coarsely grated Red Leicester cheese
225 g (8 oz) shallots, finely shredded	40 g (1½ oz) crumbled Gorgonzola cheese
400 g (14 oz) arborio rice	40 g (1½ oz) diced mozzarella cheese
Salt and freshly ground black pepper	Snipped fresh chives, to garnish

1 Pour the stock into a saucepan and bring to the boil. Reduce the heat to a gentle simmer.

2 Meanwhile, melt the butter and gently fry the shallots for 2 to 3 minutes until softened but not browned. Stir in the rice and cook, stirring, for 2 minutes, until the rice is well-coated in the butter.

3 Add a ladleful of stock and cook gently, stirring, until absorbed. Continue adding the stock, ladle by ladle, until the mixture becomes thick, creamy, and the rice is tender. This will take about 25 minutes and should not be hurried. Season well.

4 Just before serving, gently mix in the cheeses. Sprinkle with chives and serve immediately before the cheeses completely melt.

spinach & gorgonzola risotto

THE DELICATE, EARTHY FLAVOUR OF SPINACH COMBINES
PERFECTLY WITH THE RICHNESS OF GORGONZOLA,
THE ITALIAN BLUE CHEESE.

1 kg (2 lb) fresh young spinach, trimmed	400 g (14 oz) arborio rice
1.25 l (2 pts) vegetable stock	Salt and freshly ground black pepper
50 g (2 oz) butter	50 g (2 oz) diced Gorgonzola cheese
1 bunch spring onions, trimmed and finely chopped	2 Tbsp chopped fresh chives
	Shredded spring onion, to garnish

1 Wash the spinach and place in a large saucepan while still wet. Cover and cook for 4 to 5 minutes until wilted. There will be sufficient water on the spinach from washing to steam the leaves. Reserving any cooking liquid, drain well, then chop.

2 Pour the stock into a saucepan and bring to the boil. Reduce the heat to a gentle simmer.

3 Meanwhile, melt the butter in a large saucepan and gently fry the spring onions for 2 to 3 minutes until softened but not browned. Stir in the rice and cook, stirring, for 2 minutes until the rice is well-coated in the onion mixture. Season well.

4 Add the spinach cooking water and cook gently, stirring, until absorbed. Add the stock ladle by ladle, until all the liquid is absorbed and the rice is thick, creamy and tender. Keep the heat moderate. This will take about 25 minutes.

5 Stir in the spinach, the Gorgonzola cheese and chopped chives. Adjust the seasoning if necessary. Garnish and serve.

OPPOSITE **SPINACH AND GORGONZOLA RISOTTO**

saffron, pepper & marsala risotto

THIS COLOURFUL AND FRAGRANT RISOTTO HAS THE ADDED SWEETNESS OF PEPPERS AND MARSALA.

2 medium red peppers

2 medium yellow peppers

2 medium green peppers

4 Tbsp Marsala wine

1.25 l (2 pts) vegetable stock

2 Tbsp olive oil

1 medium onion, finely chopped

400 g (14 oz) arborio rice

Large pinch saffron

Salt and freshly ground black pepper

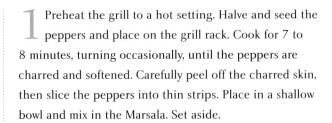

1 Preheat the grill to a hot setting. Halve and seed the peppers and place on the grill rack. Cook for 7 to 8 minutes, turning occasionally, until the peppers are charred and softened. Carefully peel off the charred skin, then slice the peppers into thin strips. Place in a shallow bowl and mix in the Marsala. Set aside.

2 Pour the stock into a saucepan and bring to the boil. Reduce the heat to a gentle simmer.

3 Meanwhile, heat the oil in a large saucepan and gently fry the onion for 2 to 3 minutes until just softened, but not browned. Add the rice and cook, stirring, for 2 minutes until coated in the onion mixture.

4 Add a ladleful of stock and cook gently, stirring, until absorbed. Continue adding the stock , ladle by ladle, until half the stock is used and the rice becomes creamy. Sprinkle in the saffron and seasoning.

5 Continue adding the stock until the risotto becomes thick and the rice is tender. This will take about 25 minutes and should not be hurried.

6 Stir in the pepper mixture and adjust the seasoning before serving.

red onion tomato risotto

FOR A SUBSTANTIAL LUNCH OR SUPPER, SERVE THIS FLAVOURFUL RISOTTO WITH FRESH CRUSTY BREAD
AND A GREEN SALAD.

75 g (3 oz) soaked sun-
  dried tomatoes

125 g (4 oz) cherry
  tomatoes, halved

950 ml (1½ pts) vegetable
  stock

50 g (2 oz) butter

2 medium red onions,
  finely chopped

2 cloves garlic, crushed

1 Tbsp lemon juice

400 g (14 oz) arborio rice

1 tsp dried or 4 tsp fresh
  mixed herbs

Salt and freshly ground
  black pepper

150 ml (¼ pt) dry white
  wine

400 g (14 oz) tin chopped
  tomatoes

1 Tbsp tomato purée

1 tsp sugar

2 Tbsp chopped fresh
  parsley

1 Reserving the liquid, drain the sun-dried tomatoes. Slice into thin strips. Preheat the grill to a hot setting and cook the cherry tomatoes for 1 to 2 minutes until lightly charred. Set aside.

2 Pour the stock into a saucepan and bring to the boil. Reduce the heat to a gentle simmer.

3 Meanwhile, melt the butter and gently fry the onion, garlic, lemon juice and sun-dried tomatoes for 2 to 3 minutes until just softened but not browned. Add the rice and cook, stirring, for 2 minutes until well-mixed. Add the herbs and season.

4 Add the wine, chopped tomatoes, tomato purée, and sugar, and cook gently, stirring, until absorbed. Ladle in the stock gradually until it is all absorbed and the rice is thick, creamy and tender. Adjust the seasoning if necessary.

5 Gently stir in the grilled cherry tomatoes and serve sprinkled with chopped parsley.

mixed vegetable & bean risotto

FOR A FILLING MEAL, THIS HEARTY RISOTTO IS THE PERFECT COMFORT FOOD ON A COLD DAY.

100 g (4 oz) trimmed and halved green beans

225 g (8 oz) shredded green cabbage

1.25 l (2 pts) vegetable stock (see method)

50 g (2 oz) butter

1 large onion, finely chopped

1 clove garlic, crushed

2 carrots, peeled and diced

2 sticks celery, trimmed and diced

400 g (14 oz) arborio rice

400-g (14-oz) tin flageolet or cannellini beans, rinsed and drained

200 g (7 oz) tin chopped tomatoes

Salt and freshly ground black pepper

1 Tbsp chopped fresh parsley

Parmesan shavings, to garnish

1 Bring a saucepan of water to the boil and cook the green beans for 3 to 4 minutes until tender; cook the cabbage for 2 to 3 minutes until tender. Reserving the cooking liquid, drain the vegetables and set aside. Use the liquid to make up the stock.

2 Pour the stock into a saucepan and bring to the boil. Reduce the heat to a gentle simmer.

3 Meanwhile, melt the butter in a large saucepan and gently fry the onion, garlic, carrot and celery for 2 to 3 minutes until softened but not browned. Add the rice and cook, stirring, for 2 minutes until the rice is well coated in the vegetable mixture.

4 Add a ladleful of stock and cook gently, stirring until absorbed. Continue adding the stock, ladle by ladle, until it is all absorbed and the rice is thick, creamy and tender. This takes about 25 minutes and should not be hurried.

5 Stir in the cooked vegetables, beans and tomatoes, and season well. Heat through, stirring occasionally, for 3 to 4 minutes until hot. Serve sprinkled with parsley and Parmesan shavings.

pilaf-style risotto

THE WARM, SPICY-SWEET MIDDLE EASTERN FLAVOURS IN THIS RISOTTO OFFER THE PERFECT ACCOMPANIMENT TO A RICH MEAT DISH.

- 1.25 l (2 pts) vegetable stock
- 1 Tbsp olive oil
- 2 Tbsp butter
- 1 medium red onion, finely chopped
- 1 Tbsp lemon juice
- 75 g (3 oz) thinly sliced ready-to-eat dried apricots
- 1 cinnamon stick, broken
- 400 g (14 oz) arborio rice
- Large pinch saffron
- Salt and freshly ground black pepper
- 3 Tbsp chopped fresh coriander
- 2 Tbsp roasted pine kernels
- 2 Tbsp sliced, roasted blanched almonds
- Fresh coriander, to garnish

1 Pour the stock into a saucepan and bring to the boil. Reduce the heat to a gentle simmer.

2 Meanwhile, heat the oil and butter in a large saucepan and gently fry the onion, lemon juice, apricots and cinnamon stick for 2 to 3 minutes until the onion is softened but not browned. Add the rice and cook, stirring, for 2 minutes until well mixed.

3 Add a ladleful of stock and cook gently, stirring, until absorbed. Continue adding the stock, ladle by ladle, until half the stock is used and the rice becomes creamy. Sprinkle in the saffron and seasoning.

4 Continue adding the stock until the risotto is creamy. This will take about 25 minutes and should not be hurried. Remove and discard the cinnamon stick.

5 Mix in the chopped coriander and adjust the seasoning if necessary. Serve sprinkled with the roasted pine kernels and nuts and garnished with coriander.

OPPOSITE **PILAF-STYLE RISOTTO**

risotto con vermicelli

AN UNUSUAL DISH COMBINING RICE, PASTA AND CREAM CHEESE. THIS NEEDS NO MORE THAN A CRISP SALAD TO MAKE A FILLING MEAL.

- 100 g (4 oz) tricolor vermicelli or spaghetti, broken into short lengths
- 1 Tbsp olive oil
- 1.25 l (2 pts) vegetable stock
- 50 g (2 oz) butter
- 1 medium onion, finely chopped
- 1 clove garlic, crushed
- 400 g (14 oz) arborio rice
- 100 g (4 oz) garlic and herb-flavoured soft cheese
- 4 Tbsp double cream
- Salt and freshly ground black pepper
- 3 Tbsp chopped fresh parsley
- One 25-g (1-oz) piece Parmesan cheese

1 Bring a saucepan of water to the boil and cook the pasta according to the package instructions. Drain well and toss immediately with the olive oil. Set aside.

2 Pour the stock into a saucepan and bring to the boil. Reduce the heat to a gentle simmer.

3 Meanwhile, melt the butter and gently fry the onion and garlic for 2 to 3 minutes until just softened but not browned. Add the rice and cook, stirring, for 2 minutes until well-coated in the onion butter.

4 Add the stock, ladle by ladle, until all the liquid has been absorbed, and the rice is thick, creamy and tender. Keep the heat moderate. This will take about 25 minutes.

5 Carefully mix in the cooked pasta, soft cheese, cream and seasoning. Stir in the parsley. Transfer to a serving dish. Garnish with Parmesan shavings.

chilli bean risotto

PACKED FULL OF THE FLAVOURS OF MEXICO, THIS VIBRANT RISOTTO MAKES A SUBSTANTIAL MAIN MEAL SERVED ON ITS OWN.

1.25 l (2 pts) vegetable
stock

2 Tbsp vegetable oil

1 large onion, finely
chopped

1 clove garlic, minced

1 green chilli, seeded and
finely chopped

2 green peppers, seeded
and diced

400 g (14 oz) arborio rice

1 tsp ground cumin

1 tsp ground coriander

1 tsp chilli powder

Salt and freshly ground
black pepper

400-g (14-oz) tin kidney
beans, drained and
rinsed

350-g (12-oz) tin corn,
drained and rinsed

4 medium tomatoes,
peeled, seeded and
chopped

1 Pour the stock into a saucepan and bring to the boil. Reduce the heat to a gentle simmer.

2 Meanwhile, heat the oil in a large saucepan and gently fry the onion, garlic, chilli and peppers for 4 to 5 minutes until softened, but not browned. Stir in the rice and cook, stirring, for 2 minutes until the rice is coated in the vegetable mixture.

3 Add a ladleful of stock and cook gently, stirring, until absorbed. Continue adding the stock ladle by ladle until half the stock is used. Stir in the spices, seasoning and kidney beans.

4 Continue adding the stock until the risotto is thick, but not sticky. This will take about 25 minutes and should not be hurried.

5 Stir in the corn and tomatoes. Mix well, adjust seasoning if necessary and serve.

oriental vegetable risotto

TRY SERVING THIS COMBINATION OF RICE AND STIR-FRIED VEGETABLES AS AN ACCOMPANIMENT TO A CHINESE MEAL. ITS DELICATE FLAVOURS ARE PERFECT TO SERVE WITH FISH OR POULTRY.

2 Tbsp vegetable oil

1 bunch spring onions, trimmed and chopped

1 medium red pepper, seeded and sliced

1 medium yellow pepper, seeded and sliced

125 g (4 oz) mangetout, trimmed

125 g (4 oz) oyster mushrooms

50 g (2 oz) bean sprouts

2 Tbsp dark soy sauce

1.25 l (2 pts) vegetable stock

2 cloves garlic, finely chopped

2.5-cm (1-in) piece fresh ginger, grated

400 g (14 oz) arborio rice

1 tsp Chinese 5-spice powder

2 tsp sesame oil

Salt and white pepper

1 Tbsp toasted sesame seeds

1 Heat one tablespoon oil in a wok or large frying pan and stir-fry the spring onions, peppers and mangetout over high heat for 2 minutes. Add the oyster mushrooms, bean sprouts and soy sauce, and stir-fry for a further minute. Set aside.

2 Pour the stock into a saucepan and bring to the boil. Reduce the heat to a gentle simmer.

3 Meanwhile, heat the remaining oil in a large saucepan and gently fry the garlic and ginger for 1 to 2 minutes until softened. Add the rice and cook, stirring, for 2 minutes until the rice is well coated.

4 Add the stock, ladle by ladle, until the stock is absorbed and the rice is thick, creamy and tender. Keep the heat moderate. This will take about 25 minutes. Stir in the 5-spice powder.

5 Fold in the stir-fried vegetables and sesame oil. Heat gently for 1 to 2 minutes until hot. Taste and season. Serve sprinkled with sesame seeds.

RISOTTO WITH MEAT

Risotto with Coriander Meatballs

Raspberry Lamb Risotto

Risotto della Carni

Chargrilled Pork with Mixed Pepper Risotto

Bacon and Spinach Risotto

Sweet Chilli and Basil Risotto

Beef Ragù Risotto

Hot Chilli Risotto

Rosemary Lamb Risotto

Risotto alla Bolognese

Basil and Pork Saffron Risotto

Fried Lamb and Broad Bean Risotto

Beef and Olive Risotto

Ham and Bean Risotto

Leek and Artichoke Ham Risotto

Beef and Broccoli Risotto

Ham and Mixed Mushroom Risotto

Persian Lamb Risotto

risotto with coriander meatballs

THE SPICY MEATBALLS ARE COOKED SEPARATELY FROM THE MAIN RISOTTO AND SERVED ON TOP OF THE RICE.

FOR THE MEATBALLS

225 g (8 oz) minced lamb

1 onion, finely chopped

1 clove garlic, crushed

1 stick celery, finely chopped

1 tsp ground cumin

1 tsp ground coriander

2 Tbsp dried apricots soaked for
   30 minutes and finely chopped

Salt and freshly ground black pepper

1 Tbsp clear honey

2 Tbsp butter

1 Tbsp oil

FOR THE RISOTTO

1.25 l (2 pts) lamb stock

50 g (2 oz) butter

1 onion, finely chopped

2 cloves garlic, crushed

400 g (14 oz) arborio rice

Salt and freshly ground black pepper

1 tsp coriander seeds, crushed

4 Tbsp chopped fresh coriander

1 Place the minced lamb, onion, garlic, celery, cumin, coriander, apricots, seasoning and honey in a mixing bowl and mix together. Roll into eight equal-sized balls and reserve.

2 Meanwhile, pour the lamb stock into a saucepan and bring to the boil. Reduce the heat to a gentle simmer.

3 Melt the butter in a large frying pan and gently cook the onion and garlic for 2 minutes until the onion has softened but not browned. Stir in the rice and cook for a further 2 minutes until the rice is well-coated in butter.

4 Add a ladleful of stock to the rice and cook, stirring, until the liquid has been absorbed. Continue adding the stock in small quantities until half of the stock has been used and the rice is creamy. Season well and add the coriander seeds.

5 Continue adding the stock until the risotto is thick but not sticky. This will take about 25 minutes.

6 Meanwhile, melt the butter with the oil in a separate pan and cook the meatballs for 10 to 15 minutes, turning, until browned and done. Drain and keep warm.

7 Stir the fresh coriander into the risotto and transfer to a warmed serving bowl. Arrange the meatballs on top and serve.

raspberry lamb risotto

FRUIT IS A PERFECT ACCOMPANIMENT TO LAMB AS IT COUNTERACTS SOME OF THE MEAT'S FATTINESS. RASPBERRIES ADD VIBRANT COLOUR AS WELL AS A SLIGHTLY TART FLAVOUR TO THIS DISH.

1.25 l (2 pts) lamb stock

50 g (2 oz) butter

225 g (8 oz) trimmed and cubed lean lamb

1 red onion, cut into eight

3 cloves garlic, minced

400 g (14 oz) arborio rice

Salt and freshly ground black pepper

2 Tbsp raspberry vinegar

2 Tbsp clear honey

225 g (8 oz) shredded red cabbage

100 g (4 oz) raspberries

1 tsp poppy seeds

1 Pour the stock into a saucepan and bring to the boil. Reduce the heat to a gentle simmer.

2 Meanwhile, melt the butter in a large frying pan and gently cook the lamb for 2 to 3 minutes until sealed. Add the onion and garlic and cook, stirring, for 2 minutes until the onion has softened but not browned. Stir in the rice and cook for a further 2 minutes, stirring, until the rice is well-coated in butter.

3 Add a ladleful of the stock and cook gently, stirring until the liquid has been absorbed. Continue adding stock until half of the stock has been used and the rice is creamy. Season well and add the raspberry vinegar, honey and red cabbage.

4 Continue adding the stock to the rice until the risotto is thick but not sticky, about 25 minutes. Stir in the raspberries, garnish with poppy seeds and serve in a warm bowl.

risotto della carni

THIS RECIPE USES ONE OF THE BEST-LOVED ITALIAN MEATS, PROSCIUTTO. IT HAS A DELICATE FLAVOUR AND IS PERFECT WITH THE PORK AND GARLIC-FLAVOURED MORTADELLA SAUSAGE.

950 ml (1½ pts) pork, veal or vegetable stock

300 ml (½ pt) dry white wine

50 g (2 oz) butter

150 g (5 oz) trimmed and cubed lean pork

1 onion, finely chopped

2 cloves garlic, sliced

400 g (14 oz) arborio rice

Salt and freshly ground black pepper

50 g (2 oz) prosciutto, cut into strips

175 g (6 oz) quartered mortadella slices

12 sun-dried tomatoes in oil, drained and cut into strips

2 Tbsp chopped fresh basil

2 Tbsp freshly grated Parmesan cheese

1 Pour the stock and wine into a pan and bring to the boil. Reduce the heat to a gentle simmer.

2 Meanwhile, melt the butter in a large frying pan and gently cook the pork for 2 minutes until sealed. Add the onion and garlic and cook, stirring, until the onion has softened but not browned. Stir in the rice and cook for 2 minutes, stirring, until the rice is well-coated.

3 Add a ladleful of stock and cook gently until the liquid has been absorbed. Continue to add small quantities of stock until half of the stock has been used and the rice is creamy. Season well.

4 Continue adding the stock for 20 minutes. Stir in the prosciutto and mortadella, sun-dried tomatoes and basil. Cook for a further 5 minutes until the risotto is thick but not sticky. Just before serving, stir in the cheese and serve in a warmed bowl.

char-grilled pork
with mixed bell
pepper risotto

TENDER PORK IS MARINATED IN A SPICY MARINADE
THEN BROILED, ADDING A SMOKY FLAVOR AND COLOR
TO THIS RISOTTO.

12-oz (350-g) piece lean pork fillet, halved lengthwise

2 Tbsp (25 mL) dark soy sauce

2 Tbsp (25 mL) red wine

1 Tbsp (15 mL) liquid honey

1 Tbsp (15 mL) dark brown sugar

2 cloves garlic, minced

1/2 tsp (2 mL) ground cinnamon

1 tsp (5 mL) sesame oil

FOR THE RISOTTO

5 cups (1.25 L) pork or vegetable stock

1/4 cup (50 mL) butter

1 leek, sliced

2 cloves garlic, minced

2 cups (500 mL) arborio rice

1 red bell pepper, seeded and chopped

1 green bell pepper, seeded and chopped

1 yellow bell pepper, seeded and chopped

2 tsp (10 mL) fennel seeds

1 Put the pork pieces in a shallow dish. Mix together the soy sauce, red wine, honey, brown sugar, garlic, cinnamon, and sesame oil. Pour the mixture over the pork, turning to coat completely. Leave for a few minutes. Meanwhile heat the broiler to medium and cook the pork for 20 minutes or until done. Keep warm.

2 Meanwhile, pour the stock into a large saucepan and bring to a boil. Reduce the heat to a gentle simmer. Melt the butter in a large skillet and gently fry the leek and garlic for 2 to 3 minutes until the leek is softened but not brown. Stir in the rice and cook for 2 to 3 minutes, stirring, until well-coated in butter.

3 Add a ladleful of stock and cook gently, stirring until the liquid has been absorbed. Continue adding ladlefuls of stock until half of the stock has been used and the rice is creamy.

4 Continue adding the stock for 10 minutes. Add the bell peppers and fennel seeds, stirring well. Continue to cook, adding more stock for a further 15 minutes until the risotto is thick but not sticky.

5 Remove the pork from the broiler and slice. Stir into the rice and serve in a warmed bowl.

bacon & spinach risotto

SPINACH AND BACON ARE A CLASSIC COMBINATION.
USING SMOKED BACON ADDS FLAVOUR THAT PERFECTLY
COMPLEMENTS THE SPINACH AND TOMATOES.

- 1.25 l (2 pts) vegetable stock
- 50 g (2 oz) butter
- 1 red onion, halved and sliced
- 2 cloves garlic, minced
- 150 g (5 oz) rindless smoked bacon, cut into strips
- 400 g (14 oz) arborio rice
- Salt and freshly ground
- black pepper
- Large pinch freshly grated nutmeg
- 2 tomatoes, seeded and chopped
- 175 g (6 oz) spinach, trimmed and washed
- 25 g (1 oz) freshly grated Romano cheese
- Finely pared zest of 1 lemon

1 Pour the stock into a large saucepan and bring to the boil. Reduce the heat to a gentle simmer.

2 Meanwhile, melt the butter in a large frying pan and gently fry the onion, garlic and bacon for 2 to 3 minutes until the onion has softened but not browned and the bacon is sealed. Stir in the rice and cook, stirring, for 2 minutes until the rice is well-coated.

3 Add a ladleful of stock to the pan and cook gently until absorbed. Continue to add the stock in small quantities until half of it has been used and the rice is creamy. Season well and add the nutmeg and tomatoes.

4 Continue to add the stock until the risotto becomes thick but not sticky, about 25 minutes.

5 Meanwhile, cook the spinach in a large, covered pan for a few minutes. Stir into the risotto 2 to 3 minutes before serving with the cheese and lemon zest.

OPPOSITE BACON AND SPINACH RISOTTO

sweet chilli & basil risotto

BASIL HAS A UNIQUE FLAVOUR WHICH IS CLOSELY RELATED
TO ITS FRAGRANCE. ITS OIL IS VOLATILE AND IS LOST IN
COOKING, THEREFORE IT SHOULD ONLY BE ADDED AT THE
END OF A RECIPE FOR FULL FLAVOUR.

- 950 ml (1½ pts) stock of your choice
- 50 g (2 oz) butter
- 1 Tbsp oil
- 225 g (8 oz) lean beef, trimmed and cut into strips
- 2 cloves garlic, crushed
- 2 tsp fresh ginger, chopped
- 1 tsp chilli powder
- 1 Tbsp dark soy sauce
- 1 tsp chilli sauce
- 2 Tbsp clear honey
- 400 g (14 oz) arborio rice
- Freshly ground black pepper
- 2 red chillies, seeded and sliced
- 4 spring onions, trimmed and sliced
- 4 Tbsp chopped fresh basil

1 Pour the stock into a saucepan and bring to the boil. Reduce the heat to a gentle simmer.

2 Meanwhile, melt the butter in a large frying pan with the oil and gently cook the beef for 2 to 3 minutes until sealed. Stir in the garlic, ginger, chilli powder, soy and chilli sauces, and honey. Stir in the rice and cook for 2 minutes, stirring, until the rice is well-coated in butter.

3 Add a ladleful of stock to the rice and cook, stirring, until the liquid has been absorbed. Continue to add small quantities of stock to the rice until half of the stock has been used and the rice is creamy. Season with pepper and add the red chillies, mixing well.

4 Continue adding the stock until the risotto is thick but not sticky. This should take about 25 minutes. Just before serving, stir in the spring onions and basil. Serve in a warm bowl.

beef ragù risotto

RAGÙ IS A BOLOGNESE SAUCE TYPICALLY SERVED WITH
PASTA. HERE IT MAKES A DELICIOUSLY SATISFYING MEAL.

950 ml (1½ pts) beef
  stock

300 ml (½ pt) red wine

50 g (2 oz) butter

1 tsp oil

225 g (8 oz) trimmed and
  cubed lean beef

1 large onion, cut into
  eight

1 clove garlic, crushed

400 g (14 oz) arborio rice

Salt and freshly ground
  black pepper

1 carrot, halved and sliced

2 sticks celery, sliced

1 Tbsp tomato purée

2 large tomatoes, seeded
  and chopped

1 Tbsp chopped oregano

1 Pour the stock and wine into a saucepan and bring
  to the boil. Reduce the heat to a gentle simmer.

2 Meanwhile melt the butter in a large frying pan with
  the oil and gently fry the beef over medium heat for
3 minutes, stirring, until sealed. Add the onion and garlic
and cook for 2 minutes until the onion is softened but
not browned. Stir in the rice and cook, stirring, for
2 minutes until the rice is well-coated in butter.

3 Add a ladleful of the stock and wine mixture to the
  rice and cook gently, stirring, until the liquid has
been absorbed. Continue adding small quantities of the
stock mixture until half of the stock has been used and
the rice is creamy. Season well and add the carrot, celery,
tomato purée and tomatoes.

4 Continue adding the stock mixture until the risotto
  becomes thick but not sticky, about 25 minutes.
Sprinkle in the herbs and serve in a warm bowl with warm
crusty bread and a fresh salad of mixed greens.

hot chilli risotto

THIS DISH HAS A LOT OF HEAT. IF YOU FIND IT TOO
MUCH TO HANDLE, REDUCE THE NUMBER OF CHILLIES
OR OMIT THE CHILLI POWDER.

950 ml (1½ pts) beef
  stock

2 Tbsp butter

1 Tbsp oil

225 g (8 oz) lean beef,
  trimmed and cut into
  5-cm (2-in) cubes

1 onion, finely chopped

2 cloves garlic, crushed

1 tsp chilli powder

400 g (14 oz) arborio rice

2 red chillies, seeded and
  sliced

One 400 g (14 oz) tin
  chopped tomatoes

200 g (7 oz) tinned red
  kidney beans, drained

Salt and freshly ground
  black pepper

1 Tbsp chopped oregano
  or basil

25 g (1 oz) freshly grated
  mozzarella cheese

1 Pour the stock into a saucepan and bring to the boil.
  Reduce the heat to a gentle simmer.

2 Meanwhile, melt the butter with the oil in a large
  frying pan. Gently cook the beef for 3 to 4 minutes
until sealed. Add the onion, garlic and chilli powder and
cook for 2 to 3 minutes until the onion has softened but
not browned. Stir in the rice and cook for 2 minutes,
stirring, until the rice is well-coated in butter.

3 Add a ladleful of stock and cook gently, stirring,
  until the liquid has been absorbed. Continue adding
small quantities of the stock until half of the stock has
been used and the rice is creamy. Add the chillies,
tomatoes, kidney beans and seasoning.

4 Continue adding the stock until the risotto is thick
  but not sticky, about 25 minutes.

5 Just before serving, stir in the herbs and add the
  mozzarella cheese. Serve in a warm bowl.

OPPOSITE **HOT CHILLI RISOTTO**

rosemary lamb risotto

ROSEMARY HAS A POWERFUL FLAVOUR AND SHOULD BE USED IN MODERATION. UNLIKE OTHER HERBS IT WILL WITHSTAND
COOKING AND IS USUALLY USED IN COMBINATION WITH LAMB.

1 l (1¾ pts) lamb stock

150 ml (¼ pt) rosé wine

50 g (2 oz) butter

1 Tbsp olive oil

225 g (8 oz) cubed lean lamb

1 onion, cut into eight

2 cloves garlic, sliced

400 g (14 oz) arborio rice

1 yellow pepper, seeded and chopped

1 green pepper, seeded and chopped

2 sprigs rosemary

2 tsp cumin seeds, roughly crushed

Salt and freshly ground black pepper

1 Tbsp tomato purée

Sprigs fresh rosemary

1 Pour the stock and wine into a saucepan and bring to the boil. Reduce the heat to a gentle simmer.

2 Meanwhile, melt the butter in a large frying pan with the olive oil and gently fry the lamb for 2 to 3 minutes until sealed. Add the onion and garlic and cook, stirring, for 2 minutes until the onion has softened but not browned. Stir in the rice and cook, stirring, for 2 minutes until the rice is well-coated in the butter and olive oil.

3 Add a ladleful of stock and wine mixture and cook gently, stirring, until the liquid has been absorbed. Continue to add small quantities of stock mixture until half of the liquid has been used and the rice is creamy. Add the peppers, rosemary and cumin seeds, and season well. Mix the tomato purée with a little of the hot stock and stir into the rice.

4 Continue adding the stock mixture until the risotto becomes thick but not sticky, about 25 minutes. Just before serving, remove the rosemary sprigs from the risotto and replace with fresh rosemary. Serve in a warm bowl.

risotto alla bolognese

USUALLY ASSOCIATED WITH SPAGHETTI, THE RICH SAUCE FLAVOURING THIS RISOTTO CONTAINS ALL THE CLASSIC BOLOGNESE INGREDIENTS.

950 ml (1½ pts) beef stock

150 ml (¼ pt) red wine

50 g (2 oz) butter

225 g (8 oz) minced beef or veal

2 rindless bacon slices, chopped

1 onion, finely chopped

2 cloves garlic, crushed

400 g (14 oz) arborio rice

Salt and freshly ground black pepper

2 Tbsp tomato purée

200 g (7 oz) tin chopped tomatoes

1 carrot, diced

1 stick celery, sliced

2 Tbsp chopped fresh oregano

1 Pour the stock and wine into a saucepan and bring to the boil. Reduce the heat to a gentle simmer.

2 Meanwhile, melt the butter in a large frying pan and gently cook the beef and bacon for 2 to 3 minutes until the beef is sealed. Add the onion and garlic and cook for a further 2 minutes, stirring, until the onion has softened but not browned. Stir in the rice and cook for 2 minutes, stirring, until the rice is well-coated in butter.

3 Add a ladleful of stock and wine and cook gently, stirring, until the liquid has been absorbed. Continue adding stock until half of the stock has been used and the rice is creamy. Season well and stir in the tomato purée, tomatoes, carrot and celery.

4 Continue adding the stock until the risotto becomes thick but not sticky, about 25 minutes. Stir in the oregano and serve in a warmed bowl.

basil & pork saffron risotto

SAFFRON GIVES THE RICE IN THIS RECIPE A DELICATE YELLOW COLOUR AND BITTERSWEET FLAVOUR. SAFFRON IS WIDELY USED IN RICE DISHES AROUND THE WORLD.

1.25 l (2 pts) pork or vegetable stock

50 g (2 oz) butter

225 g (8 oz) lean pork, trimmed and cut into strips

1 onion, finely chopped

2 cloves garlic, crushed

400 g (14 oz) arborio rice

Large pinch saffron

Salt and freshly ground black pepper

125 g (4 oz) baby corn, sliced

125 g (4 oz) French beans, trimmed

4 Tbsp chopped fresh basil

1 Tbsp pine kernels

2 Tbsp freshly grated Romano cheese

1 Pour the stock into a saucepan and bring to the boil. Reduce the heat to a gentle simmer.

2 Meanwhile, melt the butter in a large saucepan and gently fry the pork for 2 minutes until sealed. Add the onion and garlic and cook for 2 minutes until the onion is softened but not browned. Stir in the rice and cook, stirring, for a further 2 minutes until the rice is well-coated in butter.

3 Add a ladleful of stock and cook gently until absorbed. Continue to add small quantities of stock until half of the stock has been used and the rice is creamy. Stir in the saffron, seasoning, corn and beans.

4 Continue adding stock until the risotto is thick but not sticky, about 25 minutes. Stir in the basil, pine kernels and cheese, and serve in a warm bowl.

OPPOSITE BASIL AND PORK SAFFRON RISOTTO

fried lamb & broad bean risotto

TURMERIC IS USED IN THIS RECIPE TO DELICATELY COLOUR AND FLAVOUR THE RICE, COMPLEMENTING THE GREEN COLOUR OF THE BEANS PERFECTLY. TURMERIC IS A MEMBER OF THE GINGER FAMILY AND HAS A PUNGENT FLAVOUR AND WOODY AROMA.

950 ml (1½ pts) lamb stock

300 ml (½ pt) dry white wine

50 g (2 oz) butter

225 g (8 oz) trimmed and cubed lean lamb

1 onion, finely chopped

2 cloves garlic, crushed

400 g (14 oz) arborio rice

Juice of 1 lemon

1 Tbsp brown sugar

Pinch turmeric

Salt and freshly ground black pepper

1 tsp paprika

125 g (4 oz) shelled broad beans, thawed if frozen

2 Tbsp freshly grated Romano cheese

1 Pour the stock and wine into a saucepan and bring to the boil. Reduce the heat to a gentle simmer.

2 Meanwhile, melt the butter in a large frying pan and cook the lamb gently for 2 to 3 minutes, stirring, until sealed. Add the onion and garlic and cook for a further 2 minutes until the onion has softened but not browned. Stir in the rice, lemon, sugar and turmeric, and cook for 2 minutes, stirring, until the rice is well-coated in butter.

3 Add a ladleful of the stock to the rice and cook, stirring, until the liquid has been absorbed. Continue adding small quantities of stock to the rice until half of the stock has been used and the rice is creamy. Season well and add the paprika.

4 Cook the broad beans in boiling water for 5 minutes and drain well. Meanwhile, continue adding stock to the rice until the risotto is thick but not sticky, about 25 minutes. Just before serving, stir in the beans and cheese.

beef & olive risotto

TRY TO USE GOOD-QUALITY OLIVES WHICH HAVE BEEN
MARINATED IN GARLIC AND SPICES TO ADD EXTRA
FLAVOUR TO THIS RECIPE.

12 g (½ oz) dried porcini
  mushrooms

1.25 l (2 pts) beef stock

50 g (2 oz) butter

1 Tbsp oil

225 g (8 oz) lean beef,
  trimmed and cut into
  strips

2 leeks, sliced

3 cloves garlic, crushed

400 g (14 oz) arborio rice

Salt and freshly ground
  black pepper

75 g (3 oz) garlic-
  marinated black olives,
  drained, stoned and
  halved

75 g (3 oz) marinated
  green olives, drained,
  stoned and halved

25 g (1 oz) pimento in oil,
  drained and cut into
  strips

40 g (1½ oz) walnut halves

2 Tbsp chopped fresh
  mixed herbs such as
  basil, thyme, oregano
  and parsley

1 Soak the porcini mushrooms in warm water
according to the instructions on the package. Drain
and slice. Pour the stock into a saucepan and bring to the
boil. Reduce the heat to a gentle simmer.

2 Melt the butter in a large frying pan with the oil and
gently fry the beef for 2 to 3 minutes until sealed.
Add the leeks and garlic and cook, stirring, for 2 minutes.
Stir in the rice and cook for a further 2 minutes, stirring,
until the rice is well-coated in butter.

3 Add a ladleful of stock to the rice and cook, stirring,
until the liquid has been absorbed. Continue to add
small quantities of stock to the rice until half of the stock
has been used and the rice is creamy. Season well and stir
in the olives, mushrooms, pimento and walnuts.

4 Continue to add the stock to the pan until the
risotto is thick but not sticky, about 25 minutes.
Stir in the herbs, adjust the seasoning and serve in a
warm bowl with ciabatta or other crusty bread.

ham & bean risotto

SMOKED HAM GIVES A RICH FLAVOUR TO THIS DISH.
COMBINED WITH THE BEANS, WINE AND FRESH HERBS,
IT IS A SIMPLE, HEARTY DISH.

950 ml (1½ pts) vegetable
  stock

300 ml (½ pt) dry white
  wine

50 g (2 oz) butter

1 red onion, finely
  chopped

1 clove garlic, crushed

225 g (8 oz) diced smoked
  ham

400 g (14 oz) arborio rice

Salt and freshly ground
  black pepper

Pinch turmeric

125 g (4 oz) shelled broad
  beans, thawed if frozen

125 g (4 oz) thin French
  beans, trimmed

125 g (4 oz) tinned baby
  flageolet beans, drained

25 g (1 oz) freshly grated
  Romano cheese

1 Tbsp chopped fresh sage

1 Pour the stock and wine into a large pan and bring
to the boil. Reduce the heat to a gentle simmer.

2 Meanwhile, melt the butter in a large frying pan
and gently fry the onion, garlic and ham for 2 to
3 minutes until the onion is softened but not browned.
Stir in the rice and cook, stirring, for 2 to 3 minutes until
the rice is well-coated in butter.

3 Add a ladleful of stock to the rice and cook gently,
stirring, until the liquid has been absorbed.
Continue to add ladlefuls of stock to the rice until half
of the stock has been used and the rice is creamy.
Season well and add the turmeric.

4 Continue adding stock until the risotto becomes
thick but not sticky, about 25 minutes.

5 Meanwhile, cook the broad beans and French beans
in boiling water for 5 minutes. Five minutes before
the end of the risotto cooking time, add the boiled beans
and flageolet beans. Stir in the cheese and sage, and
serve in a warmed bowl.

OPPOSITE **HAM AND BEAN RISOTTO**

leek & artichoke ham risotto

HAM AND LEEKS ARE A GREAT COMBINATION, ESPECIALLY WHEN ENHANCED BY GRAINY MUSTARD. FOR VARIETY, ONE OF THE MANY FLAVOURED MUSTARDS NOW AVAILABLE COULD BE ADDED.

- 1.25 l (2 pts) vegetable or pork stock
- 50 g (2 oz) butter
- 3 large leeks, sliced
- 2 cloves garlic, crushed
- 150 g (5 oz) ham, trimmed and cut into strips
- 400 g (14 oz) arborio rice
- 1 Tbsp whole-grain mustard
- Salt and freshly ground black pepper
- 8 tinned artichoke hearts, drained and halved
- 25 g (1 oz) freshly grated Parmesan cheese
- 1 Tbsp chopped fresh coriander

1 Pour the stock into a large saucepan and bring to the boil. Reduce the heat to a gentle simmer.

2 Meanwhile, melt the butter in a large frying pan and gently fry the leeks, garlic and ham slices for 2 to 3 minutes until the leeks have softened. Stir in the rice and cook, stirring, for 2 minutes until the rice is well-coated in butter.

3 Add a ladleful of the stock and cook gently, stirring, until the liquid has been absorbed. Continue to add ladlefuls of stock to the rice until half of the stock has been used and the rice is creamy. Stir in the mustard and season well.

4 Continue adding the stock until the risotto is thick but not sticky, about 25 minutes. Stir in the artichoke hearts 2 to 3 minutes before the end of the cooking time. Add the cheese and coriander and serve in a warmed bowl.

OPPOSITE LEEK AND ARTICHOKE HAM RISOTTO

beef & broccoli risotto

BEEF AND BROCCOLI ARE WIDELY USED IN CHINESE COOKERY. IN THIS RECIPE, SOY SAUCE, SHERRY, SUGAR AND FENNEL ARE USED TO GIVE A SUBTLE ORIENTAL FLAVOUR.

- 1.25 l (2 pts) beef stock
- 50 g (2 oz) butter
- 225 g (8 oz) lean beef, trimmed and cut into thin strips
- 1 onion, halved and sliced
- 2 cloves garlic, crushed
- 3 Tbsp light soy sauce
- 2 Tbsp dry sherry
- 1 tsp brown sugar
- 40 g (1 ½ oz) blanched almonds
- 400 g (14 oz) arborio rice
- Freshly ground black pepper
- 2 tsp fennel seeds
- 175 g (6 oz) broccoli florets
- 2 Tbsp freshly grated Parmesan cheese

1 Pour the stock into a saucepan and bring to the boil. Reduce the heat to a gentle simmer.

2 Meanwhile, melt the butter in a large frying pan and sauté the beef for 2 minutes until sealed. Add the onion and garlic and cook, stirring, for 2 minutes until the onion has softened but not browned. Stir in the soy sauce, sherry, sugar and almonds and cook for 2 minutes. Stir in the rice and cook, stirring, for a further 2 minutes until the rice is well-coated in butter.

3 Add a ladleful of stock and cook, stirring, until the liquid has been absorbed. Continue to add small quantities of the stock until half of the stock has been used and the rice is creamy. Season well with pepper and add the fennel seeds.

4 Continue adding the stock until the risotto is thick but not sticky, about 25 minutes. Meanwhile cook the broccoli in boiling water for 5 minutes, then drain well. Stir the broccoli and cheese into the risotto and serve in a warm bowl.

ham & mixed mushroom risotto

PORCINI MUSHROOMS ARE MUCH SOUGHT-AFTER FOR THEIR EARTHY, NUTTY FLAVOUR. THEY ARE AVAILABLE DRIED, AND ARE SIMPLY SOFTENED IN HOT WATER FOR USE IN SMALL QUANTITIES IN MANY CLASSIC RECIPES.

12 g (½ oz) dried porcini mushrooms

750 ml (1¼ pts) vegetable stock

300 ml (½ pt) dry white wine

75 g (3 oz) butter

1 onion, finely chopped

3 cloves garlic, crushed

175 g (6 oz) chestnut mushrooms, wiped and sliced

175 g (6 oz) baby button mushrooms, wiped

400 g (14 oz) arborio rice

Salt and freshly ground black pepper

175 g (6 oz) oyster mushrooms

50 g (2 oz) Parma ham, cut into strips

1 Tbsp chopped fresh parsley or thyme

2 Tbsp freshly grated Parmesan cheese

1 Soak the porcini mushrooms in warm water according to the instructions on the package, then thinly slice. Reserve the soaking liquid.

2 Pour the stock and wine into a large saucepan and bring to the boil. Reduce the heat to a gentle simmer.

3 Meanwhile, melt the butter in a large frying pan and gently fry the onion and garlic for 2 to 3 minutes until softened but not browned. Add all the mushrooms except the oyster mushrooms and cook for a further 2 minutes, stirring.

4 Add the rice and porcini with soaking liquid, stirring, until the liquid has been absorbed. Stir in a ladleful of stock and wine mixture. Cook gently until absorbed and continue to add ladlefuls of stock until half of the stock has been used and the rice is creamy. Season well.

5 Continue to add the stock in small quantities until the risotto becomes thick but not sticky, about 25 minutes. Five minutes before the end of the cooking time, stir in the oyster mushrooms and Parma ham.

6 Just before serving, stir in the herbs and cheese, adjust seasoning and serve in a warm bowl.

persian lamb risotto

CORIANDER, FRUIT AND CINNAMON ARE CLASSIC FLAVOURINGS IN PERSIAN RECIPES AND MAKE PERFECT PARTNERS FOR LAMB.

40 g (1 ½ oz) dried apricots

950 ml (1 ½ pts) lamb stock

300 ml (½ pt) dry white wine

50 g (2 oz) butter

225 g (8 oz) trimmed and cubed lean lamb

1 red onion, halved and sliced

3 cloves garlic, crushed

1 tsp fresh ginger, chopped

1 tsp ground allspice

1 tsp ground cinnamon

1 tsp ground cumin

400 g (14 oz) arborio rice

Freshly ground black pepper

40 g (1 ½ oz shelled walnut halves

2 Tbsp chopped fresh coriander

1 Soak the apricots in warm water for 30 minutes. Reserving the liquid, drain and chop the apricots. Set aside. Add the liquid to the stock and wine and pour into a saucepan. Bring to the boil, then reduce the heat to a gentle simmer.

2 Meanwhile, melt the butter in a large frying pan and gently fry the lamb for 2 to 3 minutes until sealed. Add the onion and garlic and cook for 2 minutes until the onion is softened but not browned. Stir in the spices and cook 1 minute, stirring.

3 Add the rice and cook for 2 minutes, stirring, until the rice is well-coated in butter. Add a ladleful of the stock and cook, stirring, until the liquid is absorbed. Continue to add small quantities of the stock to the rice until half of the stock has been used and the rice is creamy. Season well with pepper.

4 Continue adding the stock until the risotto is thick but not sticky, about 25 minutes. Stir in the apricots, walnuts and coriander and serve in a warm bowl with hot bread.

RISOTTO WITH POULTRY

Chicken and Corn Risotto with Croûtons

Chicken and Tarragon Mushroom Risotto

Smoked Chicken and Mango Risotto

Chicken Asparagus Risotto

Chicken and Artichoke Risotto

Risotto alla Cacciatore

Chicken with Caramelized Apple and
Brandy Risotto

Coq au Vin Risotto

Lemon-chicken Risotto

Creamy Spinach and Chicken Risotto

Chinese Chicken Risotto

Chicken and Ginger Risotto

Chicken and Courgette Risotto

Thai Coconut Risotto

Chicken, Cardamom and Cashew Risotto

Duck and Blackberry Risotto

Duck and Orange Risotto

Duck, Pomegranate and Wild Rice Risotto

Turkey and Prosciutto Risotto

chicken & corn risotto with croûtons

THIS RECIPE IS MADE EXTRA-SPECIAL WITH GARLIC CROÛTONS WHICH ADD EXTRA CRUNCH AND FLAVOUR.

1.25 l (2 pts) chicken stock

50 g (2 oz) butter

1 Tbsp oil

4 boneless chicken thighs, skinned and halved

1 onion, finely chopped

4 cloves garlic, crushed

400 g (14 oz) arborio rice

Salt and freshly ground black pepper

Few drops hot pepper sauce

2 tomatoes, seeded and chopped

125 g (4 oz) baby corn, halved

2 thick slices white bread, crusts removed, cubed

1 Tbsp chopped fresh coriander

2 Tbsp freshly grated Parmesan cheese

1 Pour the stock into a saucepan and bring to the boil. Reduce the heat to a gentle simmer.

2 Meanwhile, melt half of the butter in a large frying pan with the oil and cook the chicken for 5 minutes over a gentle heat until browned. Add the onion and half of the garlic and cook, stirring, for 2 minutes until the onion has softened but not browned. Stir in the rice and cook, stirring, for 2 minutes until the rice is well-coated in butter.

3 Add a ladleful of stock and cook, stirring, until the liquid is absorbed. Continue to add small quantities of stock until half of it has been used and the rice is creamy. Season and add the hot pepper sauce and tomatoes.

4 Continue adding stock until the risotto is thick but not sticky, about 25 minutes. Meanwhile, cook the corn in boiling water for 5 minutes, drain and add to the risotto. Melt the remaining butter in a frying pan, add the remaining garlic and cook the bread cubes for 2 to 3 minutes, turning until browned all over.

5 Just before serving, sprinkle the risotto with herbs, stir in the cheese, turn into a warm serving dish and top with the croûtons.

chicken & tarragon mushroom risotto

TARRAGON IS A CLASSIC FLAVOURING FOR CHICKEN. IT IS ONE OF THE SUBTLEST OF HERBS AND FORMS PART OF THE *FINES HERBES* MIXTURE.

1.25 l (2 pts) chicken stock

50 g (2 oz) butter

1 Tbsp oil

4 boneless chicken breasts, skinned

1 onion, finely chopped

2 cloves garlic, crushed

4 large open cap mushrooms, peeled and sliced

400 g (14 oz) arborio rice

1 Tbsp Dijon mustard

Salt and freshly ground black pepper

2 Tbsp chopped fresh or 1 Tbsp dried tarragon

4 Tbsp single cream

25 g (1 oz) grated Parmesan cheese

1 Pour the stock into a saucepan and bring to the boil. Reduce the heat to a gentle simmer.

2 Meanwhile, melt the butter in a large frying pan with the oil and cook the chicken for 5 minutes, turning until browned. Add the onion, garlic and mushrooms, and cook for 2 minutes until the onion has softened but not browned. Stir in the rice and cook gently, stirring, until the rice is well-coated in butter. Stir in the mustard.

3 Add a ladleful of stock to the rice and cook gently, stirring, until absorbed. Continue adding small quantities of stock to the rice until half of the stock is used and the rice is creamy. Season and add the tarragon.

4 Continue adding the stock until the risotto is thick but not sticky, about 25 minutes. Stir in the cream and cheese, and serve in a warm bowl.

smoked chicken & mango risotto

SMOKED CHICKEN HAS A WONDERFUL FLAVOUR WHICH GOES WELL WITH EXOTIC FRUITS SUCH AS MANGO.

1.25 l (2 pts) chicken stock

50 g (2 oz) butter

1 onion, cut into eight

1 clove garlic, crushed

400 g (14 oz) arborio rice

Salt and freshly ground black pepper

350 g (12 oz) smoked chicken, shredded

Few sprigs thyme

75 g (3 oz) button mushrooms, wiped and quartered

40 g (1½ oz) blanched almonds

1 large ripe mango, peeled and diced

Fresh sprigs thyme, to garnish

1 Pour the stock into a saucepan and bring to the boil. Reduce the heat to a gentle simmer.

2 Meanwhile, melt the butter in a large frying pan and gently cook the onion and garlic for 2 minutes, stirring, until the onion has softened but not browned. Stir in the rice and cook, stirring, for a further 2 minutes until the rice is well-coated in butter.

3 Add a ladleful of stock and cook gently, stirring, until the liquid has been absorbed. Continue adding small quantities of stock until half of it has been used and the rice is creamy. Season and add the chicken, thyme sprigs, mushrooms and almonds.

4 Continue adding stock until the risotto becomes thick but not sticky, about 25 minutes. Gently stir in the mango pieces and fresh thyme. Serve in a warm bowl.

chicken asparagus risotto

TENDER ASPARAGUS IS PERFECT WITH DELICATELY FLAVOURED CHICKEN. TRY TO USE YOUNG ASPARAGUS SPEARS AND AVOID ANY TOUGH, LARGE SPEARS.

950 ml (1½ pts) chicken stock

300 ml (½ pt) dry white wine

50 g (2 oz) butter

350 g (12 oz) lean chicken meat, skinned and cut into strips

1 onion, finely chopped

2 cloves garlic, crushed

400 g (14 oz) arborio rice

Salt and freshly ground black pepper

Large pinch saffron

125 g (4 oz) small asparagus tips

12 g (½ oz) freshly grated Parmesan cheese

1 Pour the stock and wine into a saucepan and bring to the boil. Reduce the heat to a gentle simmer.

2 Meanwhile, melt the butter in a large frying pan and gently cook the chicken for 2 to 3 minutes, stirring, until browned. Add the onion and garlic and cook for 2 minutes until the onion has softened but not browned. Stir in the rice and cook for a further 2 minutes until the rice is well-coated in butter.

3 Add a ladleful of stock to the rice and cook gently, stirring, until absorbed. Continue adding stock to the rice until half of the stock has been used and the rice is creamy. Season well and add the saffron.

4 Continue adding stock until the risotto is thick but not sticky, about 25 minutes. Meanwhile, cook the asparagus tips in boiling water for 5 minutes. Drain well and stir into the risotto with the cheese and serve.

OPPOSITE SMOKED CHICKEN AND MANGO RISOTTO

chicken & artichoke risotto

ARTICHOKES ARE A TYPE OF THISTLE, AND ARE QUITE AWKWARD TO EAT ALTHOUGH THE TASTE IS WORTH IT. FOR SIMPLICITY, USE EITHER PREPARED ARTICHOKE HEARTS IN FLAVOURED OIL OR TINNED ARTICHOKES.

1 l (1¾ pts) chicken stock

150 ml (¼ pt) dry white wine

50 g (2 oz) butter

1 Tbsp oil

4 boneless, skinned chicken breasts

1 onion, finely chopped

2 cloves garlic, crushed

400 g (14 oz) arborio rice

Salt and freshly ground black pepper

Juice of 1 lemon

1 stick celery, chopped

8 artichokes in oil, drained and halved

2 Tbsp pimientos in brine, drained and cut into strips

3 Tbsp chopped fresh mixed herbs

3 Tbsp freshly grated Parmesan cheese

1 Pour the stock and wine into a saucepan and bring to the boil. Reduce the heat to a gentle simmer

2 Meanwhile, melt the butter in a large frying pan with the oil and cook the chicken gently for 5 minutes, turning until browned. Add the onion and garlic and cook for 2 minutes, stirring, until the onion has softened but not browned. Stir in the rice and cook, stirring, for 2 minutes until the rice is well-coated in butter.

3 Add a ladleful of stock and wine and cook gently, stirring, until all of the liquid is absorbed. Continue adding small quantities of stock mixture until half of the stock has been used and the rice is creamy. Season and add the lemon juice and celery.

4 Continue adding stock for a further 20 minutes. Stir in the artichokes and pimientos. Continue cooking for a further 5 minutes, adding stock until the risotto is thick but not sticky.

5 Just before serving, stir in the herbs and cheese, and serve the risotto in a warm bowl.

risotto alla cacciatora

THIS RECIPE COMBINES THE FLAVOURS OF FRESH LEMON, WINE, TOMATOES, MUSHROOMS AND COGNAC TO GIVE A DELICIOUS RISOTTO, PERFECT WITH TENDER CHICKEN.

4 chicken breast fillets	400 g (14 oz) arborio rice
1/2 lemon	Salt and freshly ground black pepper
750 ml (1 3/4 pts) chicken stock	
150 ml (1/4 pt) dry white wine	400 g (14 oz) tin chopped tomatoes and their juice
50 g (2 oz) butter	150 g (5 oz) button mushrooms, wiped and sliced
1 Tbsp oil	
1 onion, finely chopped	2 Tbsp cognac
1 clove garlic, crushed	2 Tbsp chopped fresh parsley

1 Rub the chicken with the lemon, and reserve. Pour the stock and wine into a saucepan and bring to the boil. Reduce the heat to a simmer.

2 Meanwhile, melt the butter in a large frying pan with the oil. Gently fry the chicken for 5 minutes, turning until browned. Add the onion and garlic and cook for 2 minutes until the onion has softened but not browned. Add the rice and cook, stirring, until the rice is well-coated in butter.

3 Add a ladleful of stock and wine and cook gently, stirring, until the liquid is absorbed. Continue adding stock until half of it has been used and the rice is creamy. Season and stir in the tomatoes and mushrooms.

4 Continue adding stock until the risotto is thick but not sticky, about 25 minutes. Stir in the cognac and parsley and serve in a warm bowl.

OPPOSITE **RISOTTO ALLA CACCIATORA**

chicken with caramelized apple & brandy risotto

COOKING THE APPLE SLICES IN BUTTER AND BROWN SUGAR GIVES THEM A CARAMEL FLAVOR WHICH COMPLEMENTS THE SIMPLE TASTE OF THE RISOTTO. DO NOT OVERCOOK THE APPLES AS THEY WILL BREAK UP AND LOSE THEIR TEXTURE.

1.25 l (2 pts) chicken stock	400 g (14 oz) arborio rice
75 g (3 oz) butter	Salt and freshly ground black pepper
1 Tbsp oil	1 Tbsp dark brown sugar
225 g (8 oz) lean skinless chicken, cut into chunks	2 eating apples, peeled, cored and sliced
1 onion, cut into eight	2 Tbsp cognac
1 clove garlic, crushed	2 Tbsp chopped fresh parsley

1 Pour the stock into a saucepan and bring to the boil. Reduce the heat to a simmer.

2 Meanwhile, melt 50 grams (2 ounces) of the butter with the oil in a large frying pan and gently cook the chicken for 3 minutes, stirring, until browned. Add the onion and garlic and cook for 3 minutes, stirring. Stir in the rice and cook for a further 2 minutes, stirring, until the rice is well-coated in butter and oil.

3 Add a ladleful of stock to the rice and cook, stirring, until absorbed. Continue adding small quantities of stock until half of it has been used and the rice is creamy. Season well.

4 Continue adding stock until the risotto is thick but not sticky, about 25 minutes. About 5 minutes before the rice is cooked, melt the remaining butter in a separate pan, add the brown sugar and cook the apples, stirring, until browned. Stir the cognac, apples and pan juices, and herbs into the risotto. Serve in a warm dish.

coq au vin risotto

ENSURE THAT THE CHICKEN IS THOROUGHLY COOKED, BY TURNING DURING COOKING AND TESTING TO SEE IF THE JUICES RUN CLEAR FROM THE THICKEST PART OF THE CHICKEN PIECE. IF LARGE PIECES OF CHICKEN ARE TO BE USED, COOK SEPARATELY IN THE OVEN AND SERVE WITH THE RISOTTO.

1 l (1¾ pts) chicken stock

150 ml (¼ pt) red wine

75 g (3 oz) butter

1 Tbsp oil

350 g (12 oz) chicken pieces

4 rashers rindless smoked back bacon, chopped

12 small pickling onions

2 cloves garlic, crushed

400 g (14 oz) arborio rice

Bouquet garni (parsley, thyme and bay leaf)

1 tsp red wine vinegar

1 tsp sugar

150 g (5 oz) button mushrooms, wiped

4 slices white bread, crusts removed and cut into triangles

1 Pour the stock and wine into a saucepan and bring to the boil. Reduce the heat to a gentle simmer.

2 Meanwhile, melt 50 grams (2 ounces) of the butter in a large frying pan with the oil and gently fry the chicken for 5 minutes, turning until browned. Add the bacon, onions and half of the garlic and cook, stirring, for 2 minutes. Stir in the rice, and cook for a further 2 minutes, stirring, until the rice is well-coated in butter.

3 Add a ladleful of stock mixture to the rice and cook gently, stirring, until absorbed. Continue adding small quantities of stock to the rice until half of the stock has been used and the rice is creamy. Season well and add the bouquet garni, vinegar, sugar and mushrooms.

4 Continue adding stock until the risotto is thick but not sticky, about 25 minutes. Meanwhile, melt the remaining butter with the rest of the garlic in a frying pan and brown the bread triangles. Serve with the risotto.

lemon-chicken risotto

LEMON CHICKEN IS A FAVOURITE CHINESE DISH. HERE IT TAKES ON A DIFFERENT TWIST, WITH A SLIGHT ORIENTAL FLAVOUR AND A FRESH LEMON SAUCE.

1 l (1¾ pts) chicken stock

8 chicken legs

50 g (2 oz) butter

1 Tbsp oil

2 leeks, trimmed and sliced

2 cloves garlic, crushed

400 g (14 oz) arborio rice

1 Tbsp light soy sauce

1 Tbsp cider vinegar

1 Tbsp light brown sugar

3 Tbsp dry sherry

1 Tbsp sesame oil

Juice of 1 lemon

Salt and freshly ground black pepper

1 Tbsp sesame seeds

Lemon slices, to garnish

1 Pour the stock into a saucepan and bring to the boil. Reduce the heat to a gentle simmer.

2 Meanwhile, cut two diagonal slits in each of the chicken legs. Melt the butter with the oil in a large frying pan and gently cook the drumsticks for 5 minutes until browned. Add the leeks and garlic and cook for 2 minutes, stirring. Stir in the rice and cook for a further 2 minutes, stirring, until well-coated in butter.

3 Mix together the soy sauce, vinegar, sugar, sherry, sesame oil and lemon juice and add to the pan. Add a ladleful of stock and cook, stirring, until absorbed. Continue adding small quantities of stock until half of the stock has been used and the rice is creamy. Season well and stir in the sesame seeds.

4 Continue adding stock until the risotto is thick but not sticky, about 25 minutes. Serve in a warm serving dish, garnished with lemon slices.

creamy spinach & chicken risotto

SPINACH REQUIRES VERY LITTLE COOKING. CHOOSE YOUNG SPINACH, RINSE, AND QUICKLY COOK IN THE WATER THAT REMAINS ON THE LEAVES. SPINACH IS PARTICULARLY GOOD SERVED WITH FRESHLY GRATED NUTMEG.

1 l (1¾ pts) chicken stock

50 g (2 oz) butter

1 Tbsp oil

350 g (12 oz) lean chicken, skinned and cut into chunks

1 onion, finely chopped

1 clove garlic, crushed

50 g (2 oz) quartered chestnut mushrooms

400 g (14 oz) arborio rice

150 ml (¼ pt) double cream

150 g (5 oz) spinach, trimmed and washed

4 Tbsp grated Parmesan cheese

½ tsp freshly grated nutmeg

1 Pour the stock into a saucepan and bring to the boil. Reduce the heat to a gentle simmer.

2 Meanwhile, melt the butter in a large frying pan with the oil and gently cook the chicken for 3 minutes turning until browned. Add the onion, garlic and mushrooms and cook for 2 minutes until the onion has softened but not browned. Stir in the rice and cook gently, stirring, until the rice is well-coated in butter.

3 Add a ladleful of stock to the rice and cook gently until absorbed. Continue adding stock to the rice in small quantities until half of the stock has been used and the rice is creamy. Stir in the double cream.

4 Continue adding the stock until the risotto is thick but not sticky, about 25 minutes. Meanwhile, cook the spinach and drain well. Stir into the risotto with the cheese and nutmeg, and serve.

chinese chicken risotto

THIS COLOURFUL DISH, FLAVOURED WITH CHINESE SPICES AND PACKED WITH VEGETABLES, IS A COMPLETE CHINESE MEAL IN ONE DISH.

1.25 l (2 pts) chicken stock

50 g (2 oz) butter

1 Tbsp oil

225 g (8 oz) lean boneless chicken, skinned and cut into strips

1 leek, sliced

2 cloves garlic, crushed

1 tsp Chinese 5-spice powder

1 piece star anise, lightly crushed

1 Tbsp light soy sauce

400 g (14 oz) arborio rice

1 carrot, cut into matchstick strips

1 red pepper and 1 green pepper, seeded and cut into matchstick strips

200-g (7-oz) tin water chestnuts, drained

75 g (3 oz) unsalted cashew nuts

25 g (1 oz) bean sprouts

1 Tbsp sesame oil

1 Pour the stock into a saucepan and bring to the boil. Reduce the heat to a gentle simmer.

2 Meanwhile, melt the butter in a large frying pan with the oil and gently cook the chicken for 2 to 3 minutes, stirring until browned. Add the leek, garlic, 5-spice powder, star anise and soy sauce. Cook for 2 minutes, stirring. Stir in the rice and cook for a further 2 minutes, stirring, until the rice is well-coated in butter.

3 Add a ladleful of stock and cook gently, stirring, until absorbed. Continue adding small quantities of rice until half of the stock has been used and the rice is creamy. Stir in the carrots, peppers and water chestnuts.

4 Continue adding stock until the risotto is thick but not sticky; this should take about 25 minutes. Stir in the cashew nuts, bean sprouts and sesame oil, and serve in a warm dish.

chicken & ginger risotto

GINGER IS CONSIDERED TO BE ONE OF THE MOST IMPORTANT SPICES IN BOTH THE EAST AND WEST. FRESH GINGER IS ESSENTIAL IN MANY RECIPES AND IS VERY DIFFERENT IN FLAVOUR TO GROUND GINGER, WHICH IS USED MAINLY IN BAKING.

1.25 l (2 pts) chicken stock

50 g (2 oz) butter

1 Tbsp oil

350 g (12 oz) lean, skinned chicken, cut into strips

1 leek, trimmed and cut into strips

2 cloves garlic, crushed

1 cm (½-inch) piece fresh ginger, chopped

400 g (14 oz) arborio rice

Salt and freshly ground black pepper

Large pinch saffron

1 courgette, cut into thin strips

225-g (8-oz) tin bamboo shoots, drained

1 Pour the stock into a saucepan and bring to the boil. Reduce the heat to a gentle simmer.

2 Meanwhile, melt the butter in a large frying pan with the oil and cook the chicken for 2 to 3 minutes, stirring, until browned. Add the leek, garlic and ginger and cook for a further 2 minutes. Add the rice and cook for 2 minutes, stirring, until the rice is well-coated in butter.

3 Add a ladleful of stock and cook gently, stirring, until the liquid has been absorbed. Continue adding stock until half of it has been used and the rice is creamy. Season and add the saffron and courgette.

4 Continue adding stock until the risotto is thick but not sticky, about 25 minutes. Stir in the bamboo shoots and spoon into a warm serving bowl.

chicken & courgette risotto

CHICKEN LEGS ARE COOKED IN A RISOTTO THAT IS COLOURED BY GRATED COURGETTE, WITH ADDED FLAVOUR AND CRUNCH FROM PECANS. IT LOOKS AS APPEALING AS IT TASTES.

1.25 l (2 pts) chicken stock

50 g (2 oz) butter

1 Tbsp oil

8 chicken legs

1 onion, finely chopped

2 cloves garlic, crushed

400 g (14 oz) arborio rice

Salt and freshly ground black pepper

3 courgettes, grated

50 g (2 oz) shelled pecan halves

25 g (1 oz) freshly grated Parmesan cheese

1 Pour the stock into a saucepan and bring to the boil. Reduce the heat to a gentle simmer.

2 Meanwhile, melt the butter in a large frying pan with the oil and gently cook the chicken for 5 minutes, turning until browned. Add the onion and garlic and cook for 2 minutes, stirring, until the onion has softened but not browned. Stir in the rice and cook, stirring, for a further 2 minutes until the rice is well-coated in butter.

3 Add a ladleful of stock to the rice and cook, stirring, until absorbed. Continue adding small quantities of stock to the rice until half of the stock has been used and the rice is creamy. Season and stir in the courgettes and pecans.

4 Continue adding the stock until the risotto is thick but not sticky, about 25 minutes. Stir in the Parmesan cheese and serve in a warm bowl.

OPPOSITE **CHICKEN AND ZUCCHINI RISOTTO**

thai coconut risotto

THAI COOKERY USES COCONUT TO FLAVOUR MANY DISHES. COUPLED WITH THE BLEND OF SPICES AND RED CHILLIES
IT MAKES A DELICIOUS MEAL.

950 ml (1½ pts) chicken
stock

50 g (2 oz) butter

300 g (10 oz) boneless,
skinned chicken, cut into
strips

1 onion, finely chopped

2 cloves garlic, crushed

1 tsp freshly chopped
lemon grass

1 tsp ground coriander

1 tsp ground cumin

1 tsp turmeric

1 tsp chilli powder

400 g (14 oz) arborio rice

2 red chillies, seeded and
sliced

300 ml (½ pt) coconut
milk

1 Tbsp chopped fresh
coriander

1 Pour the stock into a saucepan and bring to the boil. Reduce the heat to a gentle simmer.

2 Meanwhile, melt the butter in a large frying pan and cook the chicken gently for 2 to 3 minutes until sealed. Add the onion, garlic, lemon grass, ground coriander, cumin, turmeric and chilli powder and cook, stirring, for 2 minutes. Add the rice and cook, stirring, for a further 2 minutes until the rice is thoroughly coated in butter.

3 Add a ladleful of stock and cook gently, stirring, until the liquid has been absorbed. Continue adding small quantities of stock until half of the stock is used and the rice is creamy. Stir in the chillies.

4 Mix the coconut milk into the stock and continue adding until the risotto is thick but not sticky, about 25 minutes. Stir in the fresh coriander and serve in a warmed bowl.

chicken, cardamom & cashew risotto

CARDAMOM IS NATIVE TO INDIA AND HAS A SPICY-SWEET
FLAVOUR AND A PUNGENT AROMA. EITHER THE WHOLE POD
OR THE SEEDS CAN BE USED.

**1.25 l (2 pts) chicken
stock**

50 g (2 oz) butter

1 Tbsp oil

**350 g (12 oz) lean
boneless chicken,
skinned and cut into
cubes**

1 onion, sliced

2 cloves garlic, crushed

1 tsp ground cinnamon

**6 cardamom pods
or 3 tsp cardamom
seeds**

½ tsp chilli powder

1 tsp fennel seeds

**50 g (2 oz) unsalted
cashew nuts**

400 g (14 oz) arborio rice

Large pinch saffron

**Salt and freshly ground
black pepper**

65 g (2½ oz) sultanas

1 Pour the stock into a saucepan and bring to the boil.
Reduce the heat to a gentle simmer.

2 Meanwhile, melt the butter in a large frying
pan with the oil and gently fry the chicken for
5 minutes, stirring. Add the onion, garlic, cinnamon,
cardamom pods or seeds, chilli powder, fennel seeds and
cashew nuts. Cook for 2 minutes, stirring, until the onion
has softened. Add the rice and cook for 2 minutes,
stirring until the rice is well-coated in butter.

3 Add a ladleful of stock to the pan and cook, stirring,
until absorbed. Continue adding small quantities of
stock to the rice until half of the stock has been used and
the rice is creamy. Sprinkle in the saffron and season. Stir
in the sultanas.

4 Continue adding the stock until the risotto is
thick but not sticky, about 25 minutes. Serve in a
warmed bowl.

duck & blackberry risotto

BLACKBERRIES ARE A REALLY JUICY, TASTY FRUIT AND ARE BEST USED FRESH. IF FRESH BERRIES ARE UNAVAILABLE, USE FROZEN OR TINNED.

1 l (1¾ pts) chicken stock

50 g (2 oz) butter

1 Tbsp oil

4 duck breast portions

1 onion, finely chopped

1 clove garlic, crushed

400 g (14 oz) arborio rice

Salt and freshly ground black pepper

150 ml (¼ pt) dry vermouth

2 Tbsp chopped fresh thyme

100 g (4 oz) blackberries

1 Pour the stock into a saucepan and bring to the boil. Reduce the heat to a gentle simmer.

2 Meanwhile, melt the butter in a large frying pan with the oil and gently cook the duck for 5 minutes, turning until browned. Add the onion and garlic and cook for 2 minutes until the onion is softened but not browned. Stir in the rice and cook for a further 2 minutes until the rice is coated.

3 Add a ladleful of stock to the rice and cook gently, stirring, until absorbed. Continue adding stock to the rice until half of the stock has been used and the rice is creamy. Season well and add the vermouth and half of the thyme to the rice.

4 Continue adding stock until the risotto is thick but not sticky, about 25 minutes. Stir in the remaining thyme and blackberries and serve in a warmed dish.

duck & orange risotto

DUCK IS RICH FLAVOURFUL MEAT BEAUTIFULLY COMPLEMENTED BY TANGY CITRUS FRUITS.

4 duck breasts

1 Tbsp soy sauce

2 Tbsp clear honey

2 tsp ground ginger

950 ml (1½ pts) chicken
 stock

300 ml (½ pt) orange juice

50 g (2 oz) butter

1 onion, finely chopped

1 clove garlic, crushed

400 g (14 oz) arborio rice

Salt and freshly ground
 black pepper

1 large orange, peeled and
 cut into segments

2 Tbsp chopped fresh
 parsley

1 Heat the oven to 200°C/400°F/gas 6. Cut slits in the duck breasts with a knife and put on a rack over a roasting tin. Mix together the soy sauce, honey and one teaspoon ginger and brush over the duck. Roast the duck for 25 to 30 minutes until done.

2 Meanwhile, pour the stock and orange juice into a saucepan and bring to the boil. Reduce the heat to a gentle simmer.

3 Melt the butter in a large frying pan. Add the onion and garlic and cook, stirring, for 2 minutes until the onion is softened but not browned. Stir in the rice and cook, stirring, for 2 minutes until the rice is well-coated.

4 Add a ladleful of the stock and orange juice mixture and cook gently, stirring, until absorbed. Continue to add small quantities of stock to the rice until half of the stock mixture has been used and the rice is creamy. Season and add the remaining ginger.

5 Continue adding stock until the risotto is thick but not sticky, about 25 minutes. Stir in the orange segments and parsley, and serve topped with the cooked duck breasts.

duck, pomegranate & wild rice risotto

THE POMEGRANATE GROWS IN CALIFORNIA, ASIA AND MEDITERRANEAN COUNTRIES. IT IS ONE OF THE MOST ANCIENT FRUITS, WITH A WONDERFUL COLOUR AND FLAVOUR.

4 boneless duck breasts	1 onion, halved and sliced
1 Tbsp olive oil	2 cloves garlic, crushed
2 cloves garlic, crushed	400 g (14 oz) arborio rice
2 Tbsp lime juice	2 large open mushrooms, peeled and sliced
1 Tbsp acacia honey	
1 l (1¾ pts) chicken stock	Salt and freshly ground black pepper
150 ml (¼ pt) dry vermouth	Juice of 1 lime
65 g (2½ oz) wild rice	2 pomegranates, halved
50 g (2 oz) butter	Lime zest, to garnish

1 Heat the oven to 200°C/400°F/gas 6. Cut slits in one side of the duck breasts. Mix together the oil, garlic, lime juice and honey and use to brush over the duck. Cook the duck in the oven for 25 to 30 minutes, until done.

2 Meanwhile, pour the stock and vermouth into a saucepan and bring to the boil. Reduce the heat to a simmer. Heat the wild rice in a saucepan of boiling water for 10 minutes, then drain and set aside.

3 Melt the butter in a large frying pan and gently cook the onion and garlic for 2 minutes until the onion has softened but not browned. Add the arborio rice and cook, stirring, for 2 minutes until the rice is coated in butter.

4 Add the wild rice and mushrooms and a ladleful of stock. Cook, stirring, until the liquid has been absorbed. Continue adding stock until half of the stock has been used and the rice is creamy. Season and add the lime juice.

5 Continue adding stock until the risotto is thick but not sticky, about 25 minutes. Squeeze the pomegranates over a juicer and stir into the risotto; serve in a warmed bowl garnished with lime zest.

turkey & prosciutto risotto

ALL THE FLAVOURS OF ITALY ARE PACKED INTO THIS RECIPE, INCLUDING PROSCIUTTO, BLACK OLIVES, BASIL AND ITALIAN CHEESE. TRY TO USE THE LEAN WHITE MEAT AS THE RED MEAT OF TURKEY IS HIGHLY FLAVOURED.

1.25 l (2 pts) chicken stock

50 g (2 oz) butter

1 Tbsp oil

225 g (8 oz) lean turkey meat, cut into strips

1 onion, finely chopped

2 cloves garlic, crushed

400 g (14 oz) arborio rice

Freshly ground black pepper

75 g (3 oz) prosciutto, cut into strips

75 g (3 oz) stoned black olives, quartered

2 Tbsp chopped fresh basil

4 Tbsp freshly grated Romano cheese

1 Pour the stock into a saucepan and bring to the boil. Reduce the heat to a gentle simmer.

2 Melt the butter in a large frying pan with the oil and gently cook the turkey, stirring, for 2 minutes until browned. Add the onion and garlic and cook for 2 minutes, stirring, until the onion has softened but not browned. Stir in the rice and cook gently for a further 2 minutes, stirring, until the rice is well-coated in butter.

3 Add a ladleful of stock to the rice and cook, stirring, until absorbed. Continue adding small quantities of stock until half of the stock has been used and the rice is creamy. Season with black pepper.

4 Continue adding stock until the risotto is thick but not sticky, about 25 minutes. Stir in the prosciutto, olives and basil and sprinkle the cheese on top. Serve in a warm dish.

Christmas risotto

A CHRISTMAS DINNER ALL-IN-ONE RECIPE OR PERFECT FOR USING LEFTOVERS. THESE TRADITIONALLY COMPLEMENTARY INGREDIENTS MAKE A DELICIOUS DISH.

1.25 l (2 pts) chicken stock

50 g (2 oz) butter

1 Tbsp oil

225 g (8 oz) lean turkey meat, cut into strips

4 pork and herb sausages, cut into chunks

4 rashers rindless smoked bacon, chopped

1 onion, finely chopped

400 g (14 oz) arborio rice

Salt and freshly ground black pepper

4 Tbsp cranberry sauce

2 Tbsp chopped fresh sage or parsley

1 Pour the stock into a saucepan and bring to the boil. Reduce the heat to a gentle simmer.

2 Meanwhile, melt the butter in a large frying pan with the oil and gently cook the turkey, sausages and bacon for 3 minutes, stirring until the turkey has browned. Add the onion and cook, stirring, for 2 minutes until softened but not browned. Stir in the rice and cook, stirring, for 2 minutes until the rice is well-coated in the butter and oil.

3 Add a ladleful of stock to the rice and cook gently, stirring, until absorbed. Continue adding stock to the rice until half of the stock has been used and the rice is creamy. Season well and add the cranberry sauce.

4 Continue adding the stock until the risotto is thick but not sticky, about 25 minutes. Sprinkle on the herbs and serve in a warm bowl.

OPPOSITE **CHRISTMAS RISOTTO**

RISOTTO WITH GAME

Guinea Fowl with Yellow Pepper Risotto

Pheasant and Juniper Risotto

Sherried Pigeon and Peppercorn Risotto

Honeyed Quail with Lime Risotto

Creamy Quail Risotto

Venison Steaks with Lemon Risotto

Venison with Kumquat-walnut Risotto

Risotto with Venison and Mixed Peppercorns

Rabbit and Basil Risotto

Rabbit Risotto with Mustard and Prunes

guinea fowl with yellow pepper risotto

THE SWEETNESS OF YELLOW PEPPERS TAKES THE EDGE OFF THE RICHNESS OF THIS TASTY MAIN COURSE RISOTTO.
SERVE WITH A FRUIT JELLY SAUCE IF LIKED.

Four 125-g (4-oz) guinea fowl
  breasts, skinned

Salt and freshly ground black pepper

50 g (2 oz) butter

1 Tbsp olive oil

1 Tbsp vegetable stock

1.25 l (2 pts) chicken stock

2 shallots, peeled and finely chopped

2 yellow peppers, seeded and sliced

400 g (14 oz) arborio rice

150 ml (¼ pt) dry white wine

3 Tbsp double cream

2 Tbsp lemon juice

Lemon zest, to garnish

1 Season the guinea fowl breasts on both sides. Melt the butter with the oil in a frying pan until sizzling. Lay the breasts in the pan and cook for 5 minutes. Turn over and cook for a further 5 minutes or until golden and done. Remove from the pan, reserving the cooking juices, and keep warm.

2 Pour the stocks into a saucepan and bring to the boil. Reduce the heat to a gentle simmer.

3 Meanwhile, transfer the reserved cooking juices to a large pan and heat. Gently fry the shallots and yellow peppers for 2 to 3 minutes until softened. Add the rice, and cook, stirring, for 2 minutes until well-coated in the vegetable mixture.

4 Add the wine and cook gently, stirring, until absorbed. Ladle in the stock gradually until all the liquid has been absorbed and the rice is thick, creamy and tender. This will take about 25 minutes.

5 Stir in the cream and lemon juice and adjust the seasoning. Serve the risotto topped with the guinea fowl breasts, garnished with lemon zest.

pheasant & juniper risotto

JUNIPER BERRIES ADD A PUNGENT, FRESH TASTE TO THIS DISH, COMPLEMENTING THE RICHNESS OF THE PHEASANT.

Four 125-g (4-oz) pheasant breasts

Salt and freshly ground black pepper

2 Tbsp butter

1 Tbsp olive oil

2 tsp dried juniper berries, crushed

2 Tbsp dry gin

1.25 l (2 pts) chicken stock

2 medium leeks, trimmed and thinly sliced

1 large carrot, peeled and coarsely grated

400 g (14 oz) arborio rice

150 ml (¼ pt) dry white wine

Juice and zest of 1 lemon

2 Tbsp snipped fresh chives

1 Trim each pheasant breast to remove any excess sinew and skin. Leave a neat covering of skin on each. Season lightly on both sides. Melt the butter with the oil in a frying pan and gently fry the pheasant breasts, skin-side down, with the juniper berries for 5 minutes. Turn over and cook for a further 6 to 7 minutes until done. Drain, reserving the pan juices, discard the skin and flake the flesh. Place in a heatproof dish, spoon over the gin and keep warm.

2 Pour the stock into a saucepan and bring to the boil. Reduce the heat to a gentle simmer.

3 Transfer the pheasant pan juices with the juniper berries to a large pan and gently fry the leeks and carrot for 2 to 3 minutes until just softened. Add the rice and cook, stirring, for 2 minutes until well mixed.

4 Add the wine, lemon juice and zest, and cook gently, stirring, until absorbed. Ladle in the stock gradually until half the stock is used and the rice becomes creamy. Stir in the pheasant.

5 Continue adding the stock until the risotto becomes thick and the rice is tender. This will take about 25 minutes.

6 Discard the lemon zest and stir in the chives. Adjust the seasoning before serving. Serve the pheasant breasts with the risotto, garnished with a few juniper berries.

sherried pigeon & peppercorn risotto

IN THIS RECIPE, PIGEON BREAST MEAT IS SOAKED IN SHERRY AND ADDED TO A TASTY MUSHROOM
RISOTTO FLAVOURED WITH THYME.

Two 300-g (10-oz)
  pigeons, prepared

Salt and freshly ground
  black pepper

2 Tbsp butter

1 Tbsp vegetable oil

3 Tbsp medium sherry

1.25 l (2 pts) chicken
  stock

6 shallots, finely sliced

1 clove garlic, crushed

2 large mushrooms, sliced

400 g (14 oz) arborio rice

1 Tbsp chopped fresh
  thyme or 1 tsp dried

1 Tbsp pickled green
  peppercorns

Fresh thyme, to garnish

1 Slice off the legs and wings from the pigeons. Separate and pull out the wishbone. Pull the skin away from the breasts and back. Cut down either side of the breast bone to split the birds in half. Wash and pat dry. Lightly season on both sides. Melt the butter with the oil and gently fry the pigeon portions for 10 to 12 minutes, turning occasionally, until done. Drain, reserving the pan juices, and flake the pigeon flesh from the bone. Place in a heatproof dish and spoon over the sherry. Cover and keep warm.

2 Pour the stock into a saucepan and bring to the boil. Reduce the heat to a gentle simmer.

3 Transfer the reserved pigeon juices to a large pan and gently fry the shallots, garlic and mushrooms for 3 to 4 minutes until just softened. Add the rice and cook, stirring, for 2 minutes until well-mixed.

4 Add a ladleful of stock and cook gently, stirring, until absorbed. Continue ladling the stock into the rice until half the stock has been used and the rice becomes creamy. Stir in the thyme, peppercorns and pigeon flesh.

5 Continue adding the stock until the risotto becomes thick and tender. This will take about 25 minutes and should not be hurried. Adjust the seasoning and serve garnished with thyme.

honeyed quail with lime risotto

THESE LITTLE BIRDS HAVE A RICH FLAVOUR, ACCENTED IN THIS RECIPE BY TANGY LIME AND ORIENTAL INGREDIENTS.

Four 175-g (6-oz) quails

2 Tbsp butter

1 Tbsp vegetable oil

2 Tbsp clear honey

1 Tbsp dark soy sauce

1.25 l (2 pts) chicken stock

1 bunch spring onions, trimmed and shredded

1 clove garlic, finely chopped

400 g (14 oz) arborio rice

Salt and freshly ground black pepper

3 Tbsp dry sherry

Grated zest and juice of 1 lime

2 Tbsp chopped fresh coriander

Lime wedges and fresh coriander, to garnish

1 Preheat the oven to 230°C/450°F/gas 8. Wash and pat dry the quails. Melt the butter with the oil in a frying pan until sizzling, then fry the quails until browned on all sides. Drain, reserving the pan juices, and place in a roasting tin.

2 Mix one tablespoon honey with the soy sauce and brush over the quails. Bake in the hot oven for 5 minutes, turn them over, baste, and bake for a further 6 to 7 minutes until cooked through. Drain, reserving the pan juices, and keep warm.

3 Pour the stock into a saucepan and bring to the boil. Reduce the heat to a gentle simmer.

4 Transfer the reserved frying pan juices to a large pan and gently fry the spring onions and garlic for 2 to 3 minutes until softened. Add the rice and cook, stirring, for 2 minutes until well-coated in the onion mixture.

5 Season and add the sherry, the reserved roasting juices and a ladleful of stock. Cook gently, stirring, until absorbed. Continue ladling in the stock until all

the liquid is absorbed and the rice is thick, creamy and tender. Keep the heat moderate. This will take about 25 minutes.

6 Stir in the remaining honey, the lime juice and zest, and the chopped coriander. Adjust the seasoning if necessary. Serve with the roasted quail, garnished with lime zest and coriander.

creamy quail risotto

A VERY RICH CREAMY MIXTURE OF ROASTED QUAIL WITH THE FLAVOURS OF BACON, BRANDY AND RAISINS.

aFour 175-g (6-oz) quails, prepared	4 rashers rindless bacon, chopped
2 Tbsp butter	400 g (14 oz) arborio rice
1 Tbsp olive oil	Salt and freshly ground black pepper
1.25 l (2 pts) chicken stock	50 g (2 oz) seedless raisins
1 medium red onion, finely chopped	4 Tbsp brandy
1 Tbsp lemon juice	2 Tbsp double cream

1 Preheat the oven to 230°C/450°F/gas 8. Wash and pat dry the quails. Melt the butter with the oil in a frying pan until sizzling, then fry the quails until browned on all sides. Drain, reserving the pan juices, and place in a roasting tin. Bake for 5 minutes, turn over, baste, then bake for a further 6 to 7 minutes until done. Drain, reserving any juices, and keep warm.

2 Meanwhile, pour the stock into a saucepan and bring to the boil. Reduce the heat to a gentle simmer.

3 Transfer the frying pan juices to a large pan and heat. Fry the onion with the lemon juice and bacon for 4 to 5 minutes until golden. Lower the heat and add the rice. Cook, stirring, for 2 minutes until well-coated.

4 Season and add the raisins, brandy, cream and a ladleful of stock and cook gently, stirring, until absorbed. Continue ladling the stock into the rice until all the liquid is absorbed and the rice becomes thick, creamy, and tender, about 25 minutes on moderate heat.

5 Peel off the skin from the quails and discard. Flake the cooked flesh from the bones and add to the risotto. Heat through for a further 2 to 3 minutes then serve on warmed plates.

venison steaks with lemon risotto

VENISON HAS A STRONG FLAVOUR, AND IN THIS RECIPE IT IS COMPLEMENTED BY THE FRESHNESS OF LEMON AND THE DELICATE FRAGRANCE OF LEMON GRASS.

Four 150-g (5-oz) venison steaks	1.25 l (2 pts) vegetable stock
Salt and freshly ground black pepper	6 shallots, finely sliced
2 Tbsp butter	1 clove garlic, crushed
1 Tbsp olive oil	400 g (14 oz) arborio rice
Finely grated zest and juice of 1 lemon	1 stalk lemon grass, bruised
1 Tbsp clear honey	1 bunch spring onions, trimmed and shredded
	Lemon wedges, to serve

1 Season the steaks on both sides. Melt the butter with the oil in a frying pan until sizzling, and add the steaks, lemon zest and juice, and honey. Cook the steaks for 5 to 6 minutes on each side until done and richly glazed in the honey-lemon mixture. Drain, reserving the pan juices, and keep the steaks warm.

2 Pour the stock into a saucepan and bring to the boil. Reduce the heat to a gentle simmer.

3 Transfer the pan juices to a large pan and reheat. Add the shallots and garlic and cook for 2 to 3 minutes until just softened. Add the rice and lemon grass and cook, stirring, for 2 minutes until well-mixed.

4 Add a ladleful of stock and cook gently, stirring, until absorbed. Continue ladling the stock into the rice until all the liquid is absorbed and the rice is thick, creamy and tender. Keep the heat moderate. This will take about 25 minutes.

5 Discard the lemon grass. Stir in the spring onions and adjust the seasoning. Serve with the venison steaks, accompanied by lemon wedges.

venison with kumquat-walnut risotto

KUMQUATS HAVE A SHARP, CITRUS TASTE MAKING THEM IDEAL WITH RICH GAME LIKE VENISON. THIS IS A TRULY IMPRESSIVE RISOTTO.

Eight 80-g (3-oz) medallions of venison

Salt and freshly ground black pepper

2 Tbsp butter

1 Tbsp vegetable oil

125 g (4 oz) kumquats, sliced

1 Tbsp caster sugar

1.25 l (2 pts) beef stock

400 g (14 oz) arborio rice

65 g (2½ oz) walnut pieces

1 Tbsp walnut oil

4 Tbsp snipped fresh chives

1 Season the medallions lightly on both sides. Melt the butter with the oil in a frying pan until sizzling and fry the medallions over a moderate heat for 5 to 6 minutes on each side until done. Remove from the pan, reserving the juices, and keep warm.

2 Place the kumquats in a saucepan with eight tablespoons water and the sugar. Bring to the boil and simmer for 2 minutes. Set aside to cool in the liquid.

3 Pour the stock into a saucepan and bring to the boil. Reduce the heat to a gentle simmer.

4 Transfer the reserved juices to a large pan and reheat. Add the rice and cook, stirring, for 2 minutes until well-coated in the juices.

5 Add a ladleful of stock and cook gently, stirring, until absorbed. Continue ladling the stock into the rice until all the liquid has been absorbed and the rice becomes thick, creamy and tender, about 25 minutes.

6 Stir in the kumquats and their cooking liquid until absorbed. Then add the walnut pieces, walnut oil and snipped fresh chives. Adjust the seasoning and serve with the cooked venison.

risotto with venison & mixed peppercorns

PUNGENT PEPPERCORNS AND SAVOURY GAME MEATS, SUCH AS VENISON, ARE ALWAYS A DELICIOUS MATCH.

Four 150-g (5-oz) venison steaks

1 Tbsp mixed peppercorns, crushed

2 Tbsp butter

1 Tbsp olive oil

1.25 l (2 pts) beef stock

400 g (14 oz) arborio rice

4 Tbsp brandy

1 Tbsp redcurrant jelly

1 tsp pickled pink peppercorns

1 tsp pickled green peppercorns

2 Tbsp chopped fresh parsley

Salt to taste

Flat leaf parsley, to garnish

1 Rub the venison steaks on both sides with the crushed peppercorns. Melt the butter with the oil in a frying pan and fry the steaks for 10 to 12 minutes, turning occasionally, until done. Remove from the pan, reserving the juices, and keep warm.

2 Meanwhile, pour the stock into a saucepan and bring to the boil. Reduce the heat to a gentle simmer.

3 Transfer the reserved cooking juices to a large pan and reheat. Add the rice and cook, stirring, for 2 minutes until well-coated in the juices.

4 Add a ladleful of stock and cook gently, stirring, until absorbed. Continue ladling the stock into the rice until all the liquid has been absorbed and the rice is thick, creamy and tender. Keep the heat moderate. This should take about 25 minutes.

5 Stir in the brandy, redcurrant jelly, peppercorns and chopped parsley. Add salt to taste and serve with the venison steaks, garnished with parsley.

rabbit & basil risotto

THE TRULY ITALIAN FLAVOURS IN THIS DISH – PEPPERY BASIL, RICH RED WINE AND TANGY ORANGE – ARE THE PERFECT ACCOMPANIMENTS TO RABBIT.

450 g (1 lb) diced rabbit

Salt and freshly ground black pepper

2 Tbsp olive oil

1.25 l (2 pts) chicken stock

2 medium red onions, each cut into 8 portions

1 clove garlic, crushed

400 g (14 oz) arborio rice

150 ml (¼ pt) red wine

1 Tbsp dark muscovado sugar

Finely grated zest and juice of 1 small orange

Small bunch fresh basil, shredded

1 Season the rabbit with salt and pepper. Heat the oil in a large saucepan until sizzling and fry the diced rabbit for 8 to 10 minutes all over until golden brown.

2 Pour the stock into a saucepan and bring to the boil. Reduce the heat to a gentle simmer.

3 Reduce the heat under the pan with the rabbit and add the onion and garlic. Gently fry for 2 to 3 minutes until softened. Add the rice and cook, stirring, for a further 2 minutes.

4 Add the red wine and sugar and cook gently, stirring, until absorbed. Ladle the stock into the rice gradually until it is all absorbed, and the rice is thick, creamy and tender. This will take about 25 minutes.

5 Stir in the orange zest and juice. Adjust the seasoning and stir in the basil before serving.

rabbit risotto with mustard & prunes

THIS RISOTTO COMBINES RABBIT WITH RICH SHARP MUSTARD AND SWEET JUICY PRUNES.

75 g (3 oz) dried prunes

450 g (1 lb) diced rabbit

Salt and black pepper

2 Tbsp grain mustard

50 g (2 oz) butter

1 Tbsp olive oil

1.25 l (2 pts) chicken stock

6 shallots, quartered

400 g (14 oz) arborio rice

150 ml (¼ pt) dry white wine

1 Tbsp chopped fresh thyme or 1 tsp dried

Fresh thyme, to garnish

1 Soak the prunes in water to cover, until plump, approximately 30 minutes. Meanwhile, season the rabbit and coat with the mustard. Melt the butter with the oil in a large saucepan until sizzling, then fry the rabbit for 8 to 10 minutes until golden all over.

2 Pour the stock into a saucepan and bring to the boil. Reduce the heat to a gentle simmer.

3 Reduce the heat under the pan with the rabbit and gently fry the shallots for 2 to 3 minutes until just softened. Add the rice and cook, stirring, for 2 minutes until well-coated in the rabbit juices.

4 Add the wine and thyme and cook gently, stirring, until absorbed. Ladle in the stock gradually until half has been used, then add the prunes. Continue ladling in the stock until it has all been absorbed and the rice is thick, creamy and tender. This will take about 25 minutes.

5 Adjust the seasoning and serve garnished with fresh thyme.

OPPOSITE RABBIT RISOTTO WITH MUSTARD AND PRUNES

FISH RISOTTO

Filled White Fish Rolls with Mustard Risotto

Curried Fish Risotto

Chilli Monkfish Risotto

Sole and Fennel Risotto

Salmon and Caviar Risotto

Smoked Salmon and Dill Risotto

Trout and Prawn Risotto

Mackerel and Orange Risotto

Smoked Trout with Peppercorn Risotto

Colcannon Risotto

Kipper and Apple Risotto

Tuna and Harissa Risotto

Anchovy, Pepper and Tomato Risotto

filled white fish rolls with mustard risotto

PLAICE AND SOLE ARE PERFECT FLATFISH FOR FILLING AND ROLLING. BAKED SEPARATELY IN THIS RECIPE
THEY ARE FILLED WITH A SUN-DRIED TOMATO STUFFING AND SERVED ON A BED OF MUSTARD RISOTTO.

4 white plaice or other white fish fillets

FOR THE FILLING

25 g (1 oz) wholemeal breadcrumbs

1 Tbsp chopped gherkins

1 Tbsp capers

2 spring onions, finely chopped

2 Tbsp chopped sun-dried tomatoes

Salt and freshly ground black pepper

1 egg, beaten

4 Tbsp fish or vegetable stock

FOR THE RISOTTO

1.25 l (2 pts) fish or vegetable stock

50 g (2 oz) butter

1 onion, finely chopped

2 cloves garlic, crushed

400 g (14 oz) arborio rice

3 Tbsp Dijon mustard

Salt and freshly ground black pepper

2 Tbsp chopped fresh parsley

3 Tbsp freshly grated Romano cheese

1 Cut each fish fillet in half lengthwise. Combine all the stuffing ingredients except the stock, and spoon onto each fillet. Roll up the fish, starting at the wider end. Place in a shallow ovenproof dish and pour the stock around the rolls. Set aside.

2 Pour the stock for the risotto into a saucepan and bring to the boil. Reduce the heat to a gentle simmer. Preheat an oven to 200˚C/400˚F/gas 6).

3 Melt the butter in a large frying pan and gently cook the onion and garlic for 2 minutes, stirring, until the onion has softened but not browned. Stir in the rice and cook for a further 2 minutes, stirring, until the rice is well-coated . Put the fish in the hot oven and cook for 20 minutes.

4 Meanwhile, add a ladleful of stock to the rice and cook gently, stirring, until absorbed. Continue adding small quantities of stock to the rice until half of the stock has been used. Stir in the mustard and season well.

5 Continue adding stock until the risotto is thick but not sticky, about 25 minutes. Stir in the parsley and cheese. Spoon the risotto into a warmed dish and top with the hot fish rolls.

curried fish risotto

FISH AND CURRY SPICES GO VERY WELL TOGETHER. THIS CURRY IS RELATIVELY MILD AND IS ENHANCED BY
THE ADDITION OF GROUND ALMONDS FOR EXTRA FLAVOUR.

1.25 l (2 pts) fish stock

50 g (2 oz) butter

1 onion, quartered

3 cloves garlic, crushed

1 tsp ground cumin

1 tsp ground coriander

1 tsp garam masala

1 tsp chilli powder

Large pinch turmeric

400 g (14 oz) arborio rice

25 g (1 oz) ground
   almonds

Salt and freshly ground
   black pepper

3 Tbsp mango chutney

300 g (10 oz) cod fillets,
   cut into large chunks

150 ml (¼ pt) double
   cream

2 Tbsp sultanas

2 Tbsp toasted slivered
   almonds

2 Tbsp chopped fresh
   coriander

1 Pour the stock into a saucepan and bring to the boil. Reduce the heat to a gentle simmer.

2 Meanwhile, melt the butter in a large frying pan and gently cook the onion, garlic, cumin, ground coriander, garam masala, chilli powder and turmeric for 2 minutes, stirring, until the onion softens. Stir in the rice and gently cook for a further 2 minutes, stirring, until the rice is well-coated in butter.

3 Add a ladleful of stock and gently cook, stirring, until absorbed. Continue adding small quantities of stock until half has been used. Add the ground almonds, seasoning and mango chutney.

4 Continue adding stock for a further 15 minutes. Stir in the fish and cream and cook for 10 minutes, adding stock until the risotto is thick but not sticky.

5 Just before serving, stir in the sultanas, almonds and fresh coriander. Serve in a warm dish.

chilli monkfish risotto

CHILLIES AND LIMES ARE SYNONYMOUS WITH MEXICO, AND BOTH FEATURE IN THIS HOT RISOTTO DISH. FOR A MILDER
RECIPE, REDUCE THE NUMBER OF CHILLIES AND REMOVE THE SEEDS BEFORE COOKING.

1 l (1¾ pts) fish stock

50 g (2 oz) butter

1 onion, finely chopped

2 cloves garlic, crushed

1 tsp chilli powder

400 g (14 oz) arborio rice

Salt and freshly ground
black pepper

200 g (7 oz) tin chopped
tomatoes

2 green chillies, chopped

2 Tbsp tomato purée

Juice of 1 lime

350 g (12 oz) monkfish,
skinned, boned and cut
into large chunks

2 Tbsp chopped fresh basil

2 Tbsp freshly grated
Romano cheese

1 Pour the stock into a saucepan and bring to the boil.
Reduce the heat to a gentle simmer.

2 Meanwhile, melt the butter in a large frying pan and
gently cook the onion, garlic and chilli powder,
stirring, for 2 minutes until the onion has softened but
not browned. Stir in the rice and cook gently, stirring, for
a further 2 minutes until the rice is well-coated in butter.

3 Add a ladleful of stock to the rice and cook, stirring,
until absorbed. Continue adding small quantities of
stock until half has been used. Season well and add the
tomatoes, chillies, tomato purée and lime juice.

4 Continue adding stock for a further 15 minutes.
Stir in the monkfish and continue cooking and
adding stock for a further 10 minutes until the risotto is
thick but not sticky.

5 Just before serving, add the basil and cheese. Serve
in a warm dish.

sole & fennel risotto

SOLE IS A BEAUTIFUL, DELICATE FISH, SUPERB WITH FENNEL'S ANISEED FLAVOUR. IF THE FENNEL BULB IS INTACT,
USE THE FRONDS AS A GARNISH.

950 ml (1 ½ pts) fish stock

300 ml (½ pt) dry white wine

50 g (2 oz) butter

1 red onion, halved and sliced

1 clove garlic, crushed

250 g (9 oz) arborio rice

150 g (5 oz) wild rice

1 Tbsp fennel seeds

Juice and zest of 1 lime

1 bulb fennel, sliced

300 g (10 oz) sole fillets, skinned and cut into strips

2 Tbsp chopped fresh dill

2 Tbsp freshly grated Romano cheese

Lime zest, to garnish

1 Pour the stock and wine into a saucepan and bring to the boil. Reduce the heat to a gentle simmer.

2 Meanwhile, melt the butter in a large frying pan and gently cook the onion and garlic, stirring, for 2 minutes until the onion has softened. Stir in the rices and cook gently, stirring, for a further 2 minutes until the rice is well-coated in butter.

3 Add a ladleful of stock mixture to the rice and cook gently, stirring, until absorbed. Continue adding stock mixture until half has been used. Stir in the fennel seeds, lime juice and zest, and fennel slices.

4 Continue adding stock for 15 minutes. Stir in the sole and cook for a further 10 minutes, adding stock until the risotto is thick but not sticky.

5 Just before serving, add the dill and cheese. Serve in a warmed dish, garnished with lime zest.

salmon & caviar risotto

LUMPFISH CAVIAR IS USED AS A CAVIAR SUBSTITUTE IN THIS DISH. LUMPFISH ARE ABUNDANT IN COLD SEAS AND THEIR EGGS ARE COLLECTED AND DYED TO PRODUCE THIS INEXPENSIVE SUBSTITUTE FOR REAL CAVIAR.

1.25 l (2 pts) fish stock

50 g (2 oz) butter

1 onion, finely chopped

2 cloves garlic, crushed

400 g (14 oz) arborio rice

Freshly ground black pepper

350 g (12 oz) salmon fillet, skinned, boned and cut into large cubes

50-g (2-oz) jar black lumpfish caviar

2 spring onions, sliced

4 Tbsp soured cream

2 Tbsp freshly grated Parmesan cheese

1 Pour the stock into a saucepan and bring to the boil. Reduce the heat to a gentle simmer.

2 Meanwhile, melt the butter in a large frying pan and gently cook the onion and garlic, stirring, until the onion has softened but not browned. Stir in the rice and cook gently, stirring, until all of the rice is well-coated in the butter.

3 Add a ladleful of stock to the rice and cook gently, stirring, until absorbed. Continue adding small quantities of stock for a further 20 minutes. Season with black pepper.

4 Add the salmon and cook, continuing to add the stock for a further 5 minutes until the risotto is thick but not sticky. Stir in the caviar, spring onions, soured cream and cheese and serve in a warm bowl.

smoked salmon & dill risotto

SMOKED SALMON IS ENHANCED BY THE ANISEED FLAVOUR OF DILL.

950 ml (1¾ pts) fish stock

300 ml (½ pt) dry white wine

50 g (2 oz) butter

2 Tbsp lemon juice

1 red onion, cut into eight

2 cloves garlic, crushed

400 g (14 oz) arborio rice

Salt and freshly ground black pepper

1 tsp cayenne pepper

4 Tbsp chopped fresh dill

300 g (10 oz) smoked salmon, cut
   into strips

150 ml (¼ pt) single cream

Sprigs fresh dill, to garnish

1 Pour the stock and wine into a saucepan and bring to the boil. Reduce the heat to a gentle simmer.

2 Meanwhile, melt the butter in a large frying pan and add the lemon juice. Gently fry the onion and garlic, stirring, until the onion has softened but not browned. Stir in the rice and cook gently, stirring, for 2 minutes until the rice is well-coated in butter.

3 Add a ladleful of the stock and wine mixture to the rice and cook gently, stirring, until absorbed. Continue adding the stock mixture until half of the stock has been used. Season well and add the cayenne pepper.

4 Continue adding stock for a further 20 minutes. Stir in the dill, salmon and cream, and continue cooking, adding stock for a further 5 minutes until the risotto is thick but not sticky. Serve in a warm bowl, garnished with dill.

trout & prawn risotto

SMOKED TROUT HAS BEEN USED IN THIS FLAVOURFUL AND COLOURFUL DISH, BUT IF UNAVAILABLE, FRESH
TROUT FILLETS WOULD BE EQUALLY DELICIOUS.

1 l (1¾ pts) fish stock

150 ml (¼ pt) dry white
wine

50 g (2 oz) butter

1 leek, sliced

1 clove garlic, crushed

250 g (9 oz) arborio rice

150 g (5 oz) wild rice

1 green pepper, seeded
and chopped

2 tsp fennel seeds, crushed

350 g (12 oz) smoked
trout fillets, cut into
chunks

125 g (4 oz) shelled
cooked prawns

1 Tbsp chopped fresh
parsley

2 Tbsp freshly grated
Parmesan cheese

Lime wedges, to serve

1 Pour the stock and wine into a saucepan and bring
to the boil. Reduce the heat to a gentle simmer.

2 Meanwhile, melt the butter in a large frying pan and
gently cook the leek and garlic for 2 minutes,
stirring. Add the rices and cook gently, stirring, for
2 minutes until the rice is well-coated in butter.

3 Add a ladleful of stock and wine mixture to the rice
and cook gently, stirring, until absorbed. Continue
adding small quantities of stock until half of the stock
mixture has been used. Add the green pepper and
crushed fennel seeds.

4 Continue adding the stock for a further 20 minutes.
Add the fish and prawns and cook for a further
5 minutes, stirring gently, adding any remaining stock
until the risotto is thick but not sticky. Check that the
wild rice is tender; add more stock if necessary.

5 Add the parsley and cheese and serve in a warm
bowl with lime wedges.

mackerel & orange risotto

ORANGE AND MACKEREL ARE A CLASSIC COMBINATION, THE OILY FISH BEING PERFECTLY OFFSET BY
THE TANGY CITRUS FRUIT.

950 ml (1½ pts) fish stock

300 ml (½ pt) orange
   juice

50 g (2 oz) butter

1 onion, finely chopped

2 cloves garlic, crushed

400 g (14 oz) arborio rice

Salt and freshly ground
   black pepper

2 tsp fennel seeds

1 stick celery, chopped

2 mackerel, cleaned,
   gutted and halved
   lengthwise

1 Tbsp olive oil

2 oranges, peeled and cut
   into segments

1 Tbsp chopped fresh
   rosemary

1 Pour the stock and orange juice into a saucepan and bring to the boil. Reduce the heat to a gentle simmer.

2 Meanwhile, melt the butter in a large frying pan and gently cook the onion and half of the garlic for 2 minutes, stirring until the onion has softened but not browned. Stir in the rice and cook gently, stirring, for a further 2 minutes until well-coated in butter.

3 Add a ladleful of stock and juice mixture and gently cook, stirring, until absorbed. Continue adding the stock and juice until half has been used. Season and add the fennel seeds and celery.

4 Continue adding the stock mixture until the rice is thick but not sticky, about 25 minutes. Meanwhile, brush the mackerel with the remaining garlic and oil and grill for 10 minutes, turning until cooked through. Remove as many bones as possible from the fish and cut the fish into large pieces. Gently stir into the rice with the orange sections and rosemary. Serve in a warm bowl.

smoked trout with peppercorn risotto

RED RICE AND MIXED PEPPERCORNS ADD COLOUR AND FLAVOUR TO THIS RISOTTO.

1.25 l (2 pts) fish stock

50 g (2 oz) butter

1 onion, finely chopped

2 cloves garlic, crushed

1 tsp ground anise

3 Tbsp mixed peppercorns, coarsely crushed

75 g (3 oz) blanched almonds

250 g (9 oz) arborio rice

150 g (5 oz) wild rice or red Camargue rice

Salt

1 tsp almond essence

2 Tbsp chopped fresh parsley

350 g (12 oz) smoked trout fillets, cut into large chunks

2 Tbsp freshly grated Parmesan cheese

1 Pour the stock into a saucepan and bring to the boil. Reduce the heat to a gentle simmer.

2 Meanwhile, melt the butter in a large frying pan and gently cook the onion, garlic, anise, peppercorns and almonds for 2 minutes, stirring, until the onion has softened but not browned. Stir in the rices and cook gently, stirring, for 2 minutes until the rices are well-coated in butter.

3 Add a ladleful of stock to the rice and cook gently, stirring, until absorbed. Continue adding small quantities of stock until half has been used. Season with salt and stir in the almond essence.

4 Continue adding stock until the risotto is thick but not sticky, about 20 minutes. Stir in the parsley, fish and cheese and transfer to a warm serving dish.

colcannon risotto

THE TRADITIONAL RECIPE FOR COLCANNON COMES FROM IRELAND WHERE THE INGREDIENTS ARE POTATOES, CABBAGE, AND BUTTER. IN THIS VERSION, THE CABBAGE IS STIRRED INTO THE RICE, WHICH IS FLAVORED WITH FRESH HERBS AND CHEESE.

5 cups (1.25 L) fish stock

¼ cup (50 mL) butter

2 large onions, halved and sliced

1 clove garlic, minced

2 cups (500 mL) arborio rice

Salt and freshly ground black pepper

1 tsp (5 mL) freshly grated nutmeg

2 Tbsp (25 mL) chopped fresh parsley

12 oz (350 g) smoked cod, skinned and cut into large chunks

1½ cups (375 mL) shredded Savoy cabbage

¼ cup (50 mL) freshly grated Parmesan cheese

Freshly chopped parsley, to garnish

1 Pour the stock into a saucepan and bring to a boil. Reduce the heat to a gentle simmer.

2 Meanwhile, melt the butter in a large pan and gently cook the onion and garlic, stirring, for 2 minutes. Stir in the rice and cook gently, stirring, for a further 2 minutes until the rice is well-coated in butter. Add a ladleful of stock to the rice and gently cook, stirring, until absorbed. Continue adding stock until half has been used. Season well and add the nutmeg and parsley.

3 Continue adding stock for a further 15 minutes. Stir in the fish and cook for a further 10 minutes, adding stock until the risotto is thick but not sticky. Meanwhile, cook the cabbage in boiling water for 5 minutes. Drain well and stir into the risotto.

4 Just before serving, stir in the cheese and transfer to a warm serving dish. Garnish and serve.

kipper & apple risotto

KIPPERS ARE THE MOST COMMON SMOKED HERRING AND ARE USUALLY SOLD WHOLE. LOOK FOR UNDYED KIPPERS FOR THIS RECIPE.

950 ml (1½ pts) fish stock

300 ml (½ pt) apple juice or cider

50 g (2 oz) butter

8 small pickling onions, halved

1 clove garlic, crushed

400 g (14 oz) arborio rice

Freshly ground black pepper

Juice of 1 lemon

4 boned kippers, cut into strips

1 green eating apple, sliced

3 Tbsp chopped fresh sage

4 Tbsp single cream

1 Pour the stock and apple juice or cider into a saucepan and bring to the boil. Reduce the heat to a gentle simmer.

2 Meanwhile, melt the butter in a large frying pan and gently cook the onions and garlic for 2 minutes. Stir in the rice and cook gently, stirring, for a further 2 minutes until the rice is well-coated in butter.

3 Add a ladleful of stock mixture and cook gently, stirring, until absorbed. Continue adding to the rice until half has been used. Season with pepper and stir in the lemon juice.

4 Continue adding stock for a further 20 minutes. Stir in the fish, apple, sage and cream and cook for a further 5 minutes until the risotto is thick but not sticky. Serve in a warm dish.

tuna & harissa risotto

HARISSA IS A ROBUST CHILLI SAUCE, WHICH MAY BE MADE AND STORED AT HOME, BUT IT IS MORE CONVENIENT TO PURCHASE IT READY-MADE FROM MIDDLE-EASTERN SPECIALIST STORES. ALTER THE QUANTITY OF HARISSA TO YOUR LIKING.

1.25 l (2 pts) fish stock

50 g (2 oz) butter

1 onion, finely chopped

2 cloves garlic, crushed

400 g (14 oz) arborio rice

Freshly ground black pepper

1 Tbsp harissa sauce

300 g (10 oz) fresh tuna, cut into large pieces

25 g (1 oz) French beans, trimmed

40 g (1½ oz) stoned green olives

2 Tbsp freshly grated Parmesan cheese

1 Pour the stock into a saucepan and bring to the boil. Reduce the heat to a gentle simmer.

2 Meanwhile, melt the butter in a large frying pan and gently cook the onion and garlic, stirring, for 2 minutes until the onion has softened but not browned. Stir in the rice and cook for a further 2 minutes, stirring, until the rice is well-coated in butter.

3 Add a ladleful of stock to the rice and cook gently, stirring, until absorbed. Continue adding stock in small quantities until half of it has been used. Season with pepper and stir in the harissa sauce.

4 Continue adding stock for 15 minutes. Stir in the fish and beans and continue to cook for a further 10 minutes, adding stock. Stir in the olives and cheese and serve in a warm bowl.

anchovy, pepper & tomato risotto

ANCHOVIES APPEAR IN MANY ITALIAN RECIPES. THEY ARE VERY SALTY, SO DO NOT ADD ANY EXTRA SALT TO THE DISH AND CHOOSE GOOD-QUALITY FILLETS IN OLIVE OIL FOR BEST RESULTS.

1.25 l (2 pts) fish stock

50 g (2 oz) butter

1 onion, finely chopped

2 cloves garlic, crushed

400 g (14 oz) arborio rice

Freshly ground black pepper

1 red pepper, seeded and chopped

1 green pepper, seeded and chopped

2 green chillies, chopped

1 tsp (5 ml) chilli sauce

125 g (4 oz) cherry tomatoes, halved

175 g (6 oz) anchovy fillets in oil, drained

2 Tbsp chopped fresh parsley

1 Pour the stock into a saucepan and bring to the boil. Reduce the heat to a gentle simmer.

2 Meanwhile, melt the butter in a large frying pan and gently cook the onion and garlic, stirring, for 2 minutes until the onion has softened but not browned. Stir in the rice and cook gently, stirring, for a further 2 minutes until the rice is well-coated in butter.

3 Add a ladleful of stock and cook gently, stirring, until absorbed. Continue adding stock to the rice until half of the stock has been used. Season well with pepper and stir in the red and green peppers, chillies and chilli sauce.

4 Continue adding stock until the risotto is thick but not sticky, about 20 minutes. Stir in the tomatoes, anchovies and parsley, cook for a further 5 minutes and serve in a warm dish.

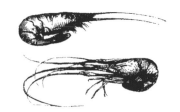

SEAFOOD RISOTTO

Sweet and Sour Shellfish Risotto

Ginger Scallop Risotto with Yellow Bean Paste

Scallop and Fennel Risotto

Red Pesto Risotto with Mussels on the Half-shell

Mussel and Prawn Risotto

Risotto with Garlic Mussels

Mussels with Bacon-saffron Risotto

Lobster Risotto

Scampi and Dill Risotto

Risotto with Flambéed Garlic Langoustine

Prawn Risotto with Sun-dried Tomatoes
and Porcini

Chilli Prawn Risotto

Oriental Crab Risotto

Mixed Seafood Saffron Risotto

Risotto Provençale

Risotto alle Vongole

sweet & sour shellfish risotto

FOR THIS ELEGANT RISOTTO, USE A MIXTURE OF COOKED SHELLFISH, SUCH AS SQUID, PRAWNS, CRAB, MUSSELS AND LOBSTER.

1.25 l (2 pts) fish stock

3 Tbsp vegetable oil

4 shallots, finely chopped

2 cloves garlic, finely chopped

400 g (14 oz) arborio rice

1 bunch spring onions, trimmed and
cut into 2.5-cm (1-in) lengths

125 g (4 oz) baby corn, sliced
lengthwise

1 red pepper, seeded and thinly sliced

350 g (12 oz) cooked mixed shellfish,
thawed if frozen

2 Tbsp light soy sauce

1 Tbsp tomato purée

2 Tbsp red wine vinegar

2 tsp sugar

2 Tbsp chopped fresh coriander

1 Pour the stock into a saucepan and bring to the boil. Reduce the heat to a gentle simmer.

2 Meanwhile, heat half the oil in a large pan and gently fry the shallots and garlic for 2 to 3 minutes until just softened, but not browned. Add the rice and cook, stirring, for 2 minutes until the rice is well-coated in the oil.

3 Add a ladleful of stock and cook gently, stirring, until all the stock is absorbed. Continue adding the stock until all the liquid is absorbed and the rice is thick, creamy and tender. Keep the heat moderate. This will take about 25 minutes. Keep warm.

4 Heat the remaining oil in a wok or large frying pan and over high heat stir-fry the spring onions, baby corn and red pepper for 1 minute. Add the shellfish and soy sauce and continue to cook for another minute. Blend together the tomato purée, vinegar and sugar and add to the wok. Stir-fry for 1 minute until the vegetables are just tender.

5 To serve, carefully mix the stir-fried shellfish and vegetables into the risotto and serve sprinkled with chopped coriander.

ginger scallop risotto with yellow bean paste

CHOOSE SMALL SCALLOPS FOR THIS RECIPE. THEY ARE SWEET AND JUICY AND REQUIRE VERY LITTLE COOKING, PERFECT FOR ORIENTAL DISHES.

1.25 l (2 pts) fish stock

2 Tbsp vegetable oil

1 bunch spring onions, peeled and chopped

1 green chilli, seeded and finely chopped

400 g (14 oz) arborio rice

450 g (1 lb) fresh scallops, cleaned and trimmed

One 2.5-cm (1-in) piece fresh ginger, peeled and cut into thin strips

1 Tbsp light soy sauce

225 g (8 oz) mangetout, trimmed and thinly sliced

2 Tbsp yellow bean paste

1 tsp caster sugar

1 Pour the stock into a saucepan and bring to the boil. Reduce the heat to a gentle simmer.

2 Meanwhile, heat one tablespoon oil in a large pan and gently fry the spring onions and chilli for 1 to 2 minutes until just softened. Add the rice and cook, stirring, for 2 minutes until the rice is coated in the mixture.

3 Add a ladleful of stock and cook gently, stirring, until absorbed. Continue ladling the stock into the rice until all the liquid is absorbed and the rice is thick, creamy and tender. Keep the heat moderate. This will take about 25 minutes. Keep warm.

4 Heat the remaining oil in a wok or large frying pan and stir-fry the scallops and ginger for 1 minute. Add the remaining ingredients and stir-fry for a further 2 to 3 minutes until the scallops are done.

5 Carefully stir the scallop mixture into the rice and serve immediately.

scallop & fennel risotto

SCALLOPS FLAVOURED WITH FENNEL AND CELERY GIVE THIS RISOTTO A DISTINCTLY SAVOURY TASTE.

2 Tbsp olive oil

450 g (1 lb) scallops, halved or quartered if large

1 tsp celery seeds

1.25 l (2 pts) fish stock

2 Tbsp butter

2 medium leeks, finely chopped

2 sticks celery, trimmed and finely chopped

1 bulb fennel, trimmed, finely sliced and fronds reserved

400 g (14 oz) arborio rice

Celery salt and freshly ground black pepper

25 g (1 oz) freshly grated Parmesan cheese

Chopped celery leaves, to garnish

1 Heat the olive oil in a large saucepan and gently fry the scallops and celery seeds for 3 to 4 minutes until done. Drain, reserving the pan juices, and keep warm.

2 Pour the stock into a saucepan and bring to the boil. Reduce the heat to a gentle simmer.

3 Melt the butter with the reserved pan juices in a large pan. Gently fry the leeks, celery and fennel for 3 to 4 minutes until just softened. Add the rice and cook, stirring, for 2 minutes until well-mixed.

4 Add a ladleful of stock and cook gently, stirring, until absorbed. Continue ladling in the stock until all the liquid has been absorbed and the rice is thick, creamy and tender. Keep the heat moderate. This will take about 25 minutes.

5 Mix in the scallops and season. Heat through for 2 minutes. Just before serving, stir in the Parmesan cheese. Serve garnished with chopped celery leaves and reserved fennel fronds.

red pesto risotto with mussels on the half-shell

THESE LARGE, MEATY NEW ZEALAND MUSSELS ARE RECOMMENDED, BUT ANY FRESH MUSSELS WILL BE DELICIOUS IN THIS RISOTTO.

1.25 l (2 pts) fish stock

2 Tbsp butter

2 cloves garlic, finely sliced

1 medium red pepper, finely diced

400 g (14 oz) arborio rice

150 ml (¼ pt) red wine

3 Tbsp red pesto sauce

Salt and freshly ground black pepper

16 cooked New Zealand mussels on the half-shell

Basil leaves, to garnish

1 Pour the stock into a saucepan and bring to the boil. Reduce the heat to a gentle simmer.

2 Meanwhile, melt the butter and gently fry the garlic and red peppers for 2 to 3 minutes until just softened. Add the rice and cook, stirring, for 2 minutes until the rice is well-coated.

3 Add the red wine and cook gently, stirring, until absorbed. Gradually ladle in the stock until half has been used and the rice becomes creamy. Stir in the pesto, seasoning and mussels.

4 Continue adding the stock until the risotto is thick and tender. Keep the heat moderate. This will take 25 minutes. Garnish and serve with crusty bread.

mussel & prawn risotto

THIS SIMPLE RISOTTO USES COOKED MUSSELS AND PRAWNS, FLAVOURED WITH DILL AND LEMON.

1.25 l (2 pts) fish stock

50 g (2 oz) butter

2 cloves garlic, crushed

400 g (14 oz) arborio rice

Finely grated zest and juice of 1 lemon

175 g (6 oz) shelled prawns, thawed if frozen

175 g (6 oz) cooked and

shelled mussels

2 Tbsp chopped fresh dill

1 Tbsp capers

Salt and freshly ground black pepper

Lemon wedges, to serve

1 Pour the stock into a saucepan and bring to the boil. Reduce the heat to a gentle simmer.

2 Meanwhile, melt the butter and gently fry the garlic and rice, stirring, for 2 minutes until the rice is well-coated in the butter.

3 Add a ladleful of the stock and cook gently, stirring, until absorbed. Continue ladling the stock into the rice until half the stock has been used and the rice becomes creamy. Stir in the lemon zest and juice, the prawns and mussels.

4 Continue adding the stock until the risotto becomes thick and tender. This will take about 25 minutes. Stir in the dill and capers. Season well and serve with lemon wedges.

risotto with garlic mussels

A TRADITIONAL COMBINATION OF MUSSELS IN THEIR SHELLS, WHITE WINE, GARLIC AND CREAM, GARNISHED WITH CHOPPED PARSLEY.

950 ml (1¾ pts) fish stock

500 ml (¾ pt) dry white wine

50 g (2 oz) butter

4 cloves garlic, crushed

6 shallots, finely chopped

400 g (14 oz) arborio rice

Salt and freshly ground black pepper

4 Tbsp chopped fresh parsley

1.4 kg (3 lb) fresh mussels in their shells, scrubbed

3 Tbsp double cream

1 Pour the stock and 300 ml (½ pint) wine into a saucepan and bring to the boil. Reduce the heat to a gentle simmer.

2 Meanwhile, melt two tablespoons butter in a large saucepan and gently fry half the garlic with the shallots for 2 to 3 minutes until softened but not browned. Add the rice and cook, stirring, for 2 minutes.

3 Add a ladleful of the stock and wine mixture and cook gently, stirring, until absorbed. Continue ladling the stock into the rice until half the stock has been used and the rice becomes creamy. Season well and stir in half the parsley.

4 Continue adding the stock until the risotto becomes thick and tender. This will take about 25 minutes. Keep warm.

5 Place the mussels in a large pan along with the cream, remaining butter and garlic, and wine. Cover with a tight-fitting lid and steam for 4 to 5 minutes over high heat, shaking the pan occasionally, until the mussels have opened. Discard any that fail to open.

6 Serve the mussels and the cooking liquid spooned over the risotto. Sprinkle with the remaining parsley.

mussels with bacon-saffron risotto

AN AROMATIC RISOTTO, PILED HIGH WITH TENDER FRESH MUSSELS, THAT IS PERFECT FOR AN INFORMAL SUPPER.

1.25 l (2 pts) fish stock

50 g (2 oz) butter

1 Tbsp olive oil

1 medium onion, finely chopped

4 rashers lean bacon, finely chopped

400 g (14 oz) arborio rice

Large pinch saffron

Salt and freshly ground black pepper

25 g (1 oz) freshly grated Parmesan cheese

2 Tbsp chopped fresh parsley

1.4 kg (3 lb) fresh mussels in their shells, scrubbed

150 ml (¼ pt) dry white wine

1 Pour the stock into a saucepan and bring to the boil. Reduce the heat to a gentle simmer.

2 Meanwhile, melt two tablespoons butter with the oil in a large pan and gently fry the onion and bacon for 2 to 3 minutes until just softened. Add the rice and cook gently, stirring, for 2 minutes until well-mixed.

3 Add a ladleful of stock and cook gently, stirring, until absorbed. Continue ladling the stock into the rice until half the stock has been used and the rice becomes creamy. Sprinkle in the saffron.

4 Continue adding the stock until the risotto becomes thick and tender. This will take about 25 minutes. Season and stir in the Parmesan cheese and half the parsley. Keep warm.

5 Place the mussels in a large saucepan with the remaining butter and the wine. Cover with a tight-fitting lid and steam over high heat for 4 to 5 minutes, shaking the pan occasionally, until the mussels have opened. Discard any that fail to open.

6 Serve the risotto with the mussels and cooking liquid spooned over. Sprinkle with remaining chopped parsley.

lobster risotto

TENDER LOBSTER IS MIXED WITH CREAM, CHEESE, HERBS AND WINE – A LUXURIOUSLY RICH RISOTTO THAT MAKES AN EXCELLENT STARTER TO A LIGHT MEAL.

950 ml (1½ pts) fish stock

300 ml (½ pt) dry white wine

2 Tbsp butter

1 Tbsp olive oil

6 shallots, shredded

1 clove garlic, crushed

400 g (14 oz) arborio rice

225 g (8 oz) cooked lobster meat, flaked

2 Tbsp chopped fresh parsley

2 Tbsp chopped fresh tarragon

2 Tbsp chopped fresh dill

4 Tbsp double cream

Salt and freshly ground black pepper

25 g (1 oz) freshly grated Parmesan cheese

1 Pour the stock and wine into a saucepan and bring to the boil. Reduce the heat to a gentle simmer.

2 Meanwhile, melt the butter with the oil in a large pan and gently fry the shallots and garlic for 2 to 3 minutes until softened but not browned. Add the rice and cook, stirring, for 2 minutes, until well-coated in the shallot mixture.

3 Add a ladleful of stock and cook gently, stirring, until absorbed. Continue ladling in the stock until half is used and the rice becomes creamy. Mix in the lobster, half the herbs and the cream.

4 Continue adding the stock until the risotto becomes thick, but not sticky. This will take about 25 minutes and should not be hurried.

5 Season. Just before serving, stir in the grated cheese and serve sprinkled with remaining herbs.

scampi & dill risotto

SCAMPI ARE VERY JUICY AND HAVE A SWEET TASTE – THEY REQUIRE VERY LITTLE COOKING. HERE THEY COMBINE WITH A WINE AND HERB RISOTTO TO MAKE A DELICIOUS SUPPER DISH.

950 ml (1½ pts) fish stock

300 ml (½ pt) plus 2 Tbsp dry white wine

50 g (2 oz) butter

4 shallots, finely chopped

2 cloves garlic, finely chopped

400 g (14 oz) arborio rice

Salt and freshly ground black pepper

2 Tbsp chopped fresh dill

450 g (1 lb) raw shelled scampi

3 Tbsp double cream

1 tsp paprika

1 Pour the stock and 300 ml (½ pint) wine into a saucepan and bring to the boil. Reduce the heat to a gentle simmer.

2 Meanwhile, melt half the butter in a large pan and gently fry the shallots and garlic for 2 to 3 minutes until softened. Add the rice and cook, stirring, for 2 minutes.

3 Add a ladleful of the stock and wine mixture and cook gently, stirring, until absorbed. Continue ladling the stock into the rice until all the stock is used and the rice becomes thick, creamy and tender. Keep the heat moderate. This will take about 25 minutes. Season well and stir in the dill. Keep warm.

4 Melt the remaining butter in a frying pan and gently fry the scampi, stirring, for 2 to 3 minutes until pink all over. Stir in the cream and the remaining wine and cook for another minute.

5 Gently mix the scampi and creamy liquid into the rice and serve sprinkled with the paprika.

risotto with flambéed garlic langoustine

LUXURIOUSLY BIG JUICY DUBLIN BAY PRAWNS AND SLIVERS OF GARLIC ARE FLAMBÉED WITH BRANDY AND STIRRED INTO A DELICATE TARRAGON RISOTTO.

1.25 l (2 pts) fish stock

50 g (2 oz) butter

1 medium leek, trimmed and finely chopped

1 bay leaf

400 g (14 oz) arborio rice

Salt and freshly ground black pepper

2 Tbsp chopped fresh tarragon

Finely grated zest of 1 lemon

3 cloves garlic, finely sliced

16 raw langoustine

3 Tbsp brandy

Fresh tarragon and lemon wedges, to garnish

1 Pour the stock into a saucepan and bring to the boil. Reduce the heat to a gentle simmer.

2 Meanwhile, melt half the butter in a large pan and gently fry the leek and bay leaf for 2 to 3 minutes until softened. Add the rice and cook, stirring, for 2 minutes until well-coated in the leek butter.

3 Add a ladleful of stock and cook gently, stirring, until absorbed. Continue ladling the stock into the rice until all the liquid has been absorbed and the rice is thick, creamy and tender. Keep the heat moderate. This will take about 25 minutes. Discard the bay leaf, season well and stir in the tarragon and lemon zest. Keep warm.

4 Melt the remaining butter in a frying pan and gently fry the garlic and prawns for 2 to 3 minutes, stirring, until the prawns are pink all over. Warm the brandy, pour over the prawns and carefully ignite using a taper. Once the flames have died down, transfer the langoustines to the risotto along with the juices. Gently mix in the juices and serve garnished with fresh tarragon and lemon wedges.

prawn risotto with sun-dried tomatoes & porcini

DRIED VEGETABLES HAVE A MORE INTENSE FLAVOUR THAN FRESH. FOR MAXIMUM SEASONING USE THE SOAKING LIQUID IN THE RISOTTO.

950 ml (1½ pts) fish stock

100 g (4 oz) sun-dried tomatoes, soaked as directed

50 g (2 oz) dried porcini mushrooms, soaked as directed

3 Tbsp olive oil

2 medium red onions, finely sliced

400 g (14 oz) arborio rice

150 ml (¼ pt) extra-dry white vermouth

Salt and freshly ground black pepper

225 g (8 oz) cooked shelled prawns, thawed if frozen

2 Tbsp chopped fresh parsley

1 Pour the stock into a saucepan and bring to the boil. Reduce the heat to a gentle simmer.

2 Meanwhile, drain the tomatoes and mushrooms, reserving the soaking liquid, and rinse well. Slice the tomatoes into thin strips, and cut up the mushrooms if large, or leave whole.

3 Heat the oil in a large saucepan and gently fry the onions, sun-dried tomatoes and mushrooms for 5 minutes until just softened, but not browned. Add the rice and cook, stirring, until the rice is coated all over in the vegetable mixture.

4 Add the dry vermouth and 150 ml (¼ pint) soaking liquid and cook gently, stirring, until absorbed. Gradually ladle in the stock until all the liquid has been absorbed and the rice becomes thick, creamy and tender. Keep the heat moderate. This will take about 25 minutes.

5 Season and stir in the prawns. Heat through for 2 minutes. Serve sprinkled with chopped parsley.

chilli prawn risotto

THIS RISOTTO HAS THE FLAVOUR OF THAILAND WITH INGREDIENTS SUCH AS CHILLIES, COCONUT, SPRING ONIONS, LEMON GRASS AND PEANUTS. IT IS AN IDEAL DISH TO SERVE ON A SPECIAL OCCASION.

950 ml (1½ pts) fish stock

1 Tbsp vegetable oil

1 bunch spring onions, trimmed and chopped

1 clove garlic, crushed

1 red chilli, seeded and finely chopped

400 g (14 oz) arborio rice

1 stalk lemon grass, bruised

300 ml (½ pt) coconut milk

1 Tbsp Thai fish sauce

225 g (8 oz) shelled large prawns, thawed if frozen

25 g (1 oz) crushed roasted peanuts

Shredded spring onions and red chilli, to garnish

1 Pour the stock into a saucepan and bring to the boil. Reduce the heat to a gentle simmer.

2 Meanwhile, heat the oil in a large saucepan and gently fry the spring onions, garlic and red chilli for 1 to 2 minutes, until just softened. Add the rice and cook, stirring, for 2 minutes until well-coated in the spring onion mixture.

3 Add the lemon grass, coconut milk and fish sauce and cook gently, stirring, until absorbed. Gradually ladle in the stock until all the liquid has been absorbed and the rice is thick, creamy and tender. Keep the heat moderate. This will take about 25 minutes.

4 Discard the lemon grass. Stir in the prawns and cook for a further 2 minutes.

5 Serve sprinkled with chopped peanuts, and garnish with spring onions and red chilli.

OPPOSITE CHILLI PRAWN RISOTTO

oriental crab risotto

CHOOSE CRAB CLAWS THAT CONTAIN A LOT OF MEAT. IF SMALLER ONES ARE AVAILABLE, THEN USE 12 TO 16 FOR THIS RECIPE.

1.25 l (2 pts) fish stock

3 Tbsp vegetable oil

1 bunch spring onions, trimmed and finely chopped

1 red pepper, seeded and sliced

1 clove garlic, finely chopped

½-in (1-cm) piece fresh ginger, finely chopped

400 g (14 oz) arborio rice

8 large crab claws, cracked

1 tsp Chinese 5-spice powder

2 Tbsp dark soy sauce

225 g (8 oz) finely shredded Chinese cabbage

2 tsp sesame oil

2 Tbsp snipped fresh chives

1 Pour the stock into a saucepan and bring to the boil. Reduce the heat to a gentle simmer.

2 Meanwhile, heat the vegetable oil in a large pan and gently fry the spring onions, red pepper, garlic and ginger for 3 to 4 minutes until softened. Add the rice and cook, stirring, for 2 minutes until well-mixed.

3 Add a ladleful of stock and cook gently, stirring, until absorbed. Continue to ladle in the stock until all the liquid is absorbed and the rice becomes thick, creamy and tender. Keep the heat moderate. This will take about 25 minutes. Keep warm.

4 Heat the remaining oil in a wok or large frying pan and stir-fry the crab claws with the 5-spice powder for 1 minute. Add the soy sauce and Chinese cabbage and stir-fry for a further 2 to 3 minutes until the leaves are tender and wilted. Mix in the sesame oil.

5 Spoon the stir-fried crab mixture over the rice and serve sprinkled with snipped chives.

mixed seafood saffron risotto

A SELECTION OF MUSSELS, CLAMS, PRAWNS AND SCALLOPS
ARE COOKED IN A WINE AND CREAM SAUCE AND SERVED
WITH A FRAGRANT, GOLDEN RISOTTO.

1.25 l (2 pts) fish stock

75 g (3 oz) butter

1 medium onion, finely
chopped

2 cloves garlic, crushed

400 g (14 oz) arborio rice

Large pinch saffron

Salt and freshly ground
black pepper

150 ml (¼ pt) dry white
wine

4 Tbsp double cream

450 g (1 lb) fresh mussels
in their shells, scrubbed

450 g (1 lb) fresh clams in
their shells, scrubbed
and soaked

225 g (8 oz) fresh scallops,
cleaned and trimmed

225 g (8 oz) large raw
prawns in their shells

2 Tbsp chopped fresh
parsley

1 Pour the stock into a saucepan and bring to the boil.
Reduce the heat to a gentle simmer.

2 Meanwhile, melt 50 grams (2 ounces) butter in a
large saucepan and gently fry the onion and half the
garlic for 2 to 3 minutes until softened but not browned.
Stir in the rice and cook, stirring, for 2 minutes until the
rice is well-coated in butter.

3 Add a ladleful of stock and cook gently, stirring,
until absorbed. Continue ladling the stock into the
rice until half the stock has been used and the rice
becomes creamy. Sprinkle in the saffron and seasoning.

4 Continue adding the stock until the risotto becomes
thick, but not sticky. This will take about 25 minutes
and should not be hurried. Keep warm.

5 Pour the wine into a saucepan and add the cream
and remaining garlic and butter. Add the shellfish,
cover with a tight-fitting lid and cook over high heat for

5 to 6 minutes, shaking the pan occasionally, until the
mussels and clams have opened and the prawns are pink.
Discard any mussels or clams that fail to open.

6 Serve the risotto with the shellfish and juices
spooned over, and sprinkle with the parsley.

risotto provençale

PACKED FULL OF THE SUNNY FLAVOURS OF THE
MEDITERRANEAN, THIS DELICIOUS RISOTTO MAKES A
SUBSTANTIAL MAIN COURSE SERVED WITH CRUSTY BREAD
AND A CRISP SALAD.

950 ml (1½ pts) fish stock

4 Tbsp olive oil

6 shallots, finely chopped

1 clove garlic, thinly sliced

1 yellow pepper, seeded
and diced

2 medium courgettes,
trimmed and diced

1 medium aubergine,
trimmed and diced

400 g (14 oz) arborio rice

1 tsp dried or 2 Tbsp fresh
mixed herbs

150 ml (¼ pt) dry red
wine

400 g (14 oz) tin chopped
tomatoes

1 tsp caster sugar

Salt and freshly ground
black pepper

225 g (8 oz) prepared
baby squid, sliced into
rings

Few stoned black olives

Fresh herbs, to garnish

1 Pour the stock into a saucepan and bring to the boil.
Reduce the heat to a gentle simmer.

2 Meanwhile, heat the oil in a large pan and gently fry
the shallots, garlic, pepper, courgette and aubergine
for 4 to 5 minutes until softened. Add the rice and cook,
stirring, for 2 minutes until well-mixed.

3 Add the herbs, wine, tomatoes and sugar and cook
gently, stirring, until absorbed. Gradually ladle in
the stock until half has been used and the rice becomes
creamy. Season well and stir in the squid.

4 Continue adding the stock until the risotto becomes
thick and tender, about 25 minutes. Sprinkle with
olives and fresh herbs, and serve.

risotto alle vongole

IN ITALY, VERY SMALL CLAMS (VONGOLE) ARE USUALLY
SERVED WITH FETTUCINE, BUT THEY ADAPT VERY WELL TO
THIS RISOTTO DISH.

1.25 l (2 pts) fish stock or
a mix of clam juice and
fish stock

2 Tbsp olive oil

3 cloves garlic, sliced

3 small dried chillies,
chopped

400 g (14 oz) arborio rice

Salt and freshly ground
black pepper

1.4 kg (3 lb) clams,
scrubbed and soaked

150 ml (¼ pt) dry white
wine

2 Tbsp chopped fresh
parsley

1 Pour the stock into a saucepan and bring to the boil.
Reduce the heat to a gentle simmer.

2 Meanwhile, heat the oil in a large pan and gently fry
two-thirds of the garlic and half the chillies for 1 to
2 minutes until just softened but not browned. Add the
rice and cook, stirring, for 2 minutes until the rice is well-
coated in the oil.

3 Add a ladleful of stock and cook gently, stirring,
until absorbed. Continue ladling in the stock until
all the liquid has been absorbed and the rice becomes
thick, creamy and tender. Keep the heat moderate. This
will take about 25 minutes. Season well and keep warm.

4 Place the clams in a large saucepan and pour over
the wine. Add the remaining garlic and chillies.
Cover with a tight-fitting lid, and cook over a high heat
until they open, shaking the pan constantly. Discard any
clams that fail to open.

5 To serve the risotto, spoon the clams with their
cooking juices over each portion of rice and
sprinkle with parsley.

OPPOSITE RISOTTO ALLE VONGOLE

SWEET RISOTTO

Chocolate and Vanilla Risotto

Chocolate Orange Risotto

Tiramisù Risotto

Cream Cheese and Apricot Risotto

Raspberry, Peach and Hazelnut Risotto

Summer Fruits Risotto

Lemon and Sultana Risotto

Sunshine Fruit Risotto

Apple, Pear and Cinnamon Risotto

chocolate & vanilla risotto

THIS IS A RICH INDULGENT DESSERT THAT IS NOT FOR THOSE COUNTING THE CALORIES.

1 l (1¾ pts) milk
50 g (2 oz) butter
400 g (14 oz) arborio rice
2 Tbsp sugar

1 vanilla pod
80 g (3 oz) plain chocolate, grated
150 ml (¼ pt) double cream

1 Pour the milk into a saucepan and bring to the boil. Reduce the heat to a gentle simmer.

2 Meanwhile, melt the butter in a large frying pan and gently cook the rice for 2 minutes, stirring, until the rice is well-coated in butter.

3 Add a ladleful of milk and cook gently, stirring until absorbed. Stir in the sugar and vanilla pod. Continue adding small quantities of milk for 20 minutes, stirring, until the milk has been used. Remove the vanilla pod from the rice.

4 Add the chocolate and cream and cook for a further 5 minutes. Serve in a warm dish.

chocolate orange risotto

CHOCOLATE AND ORANGE ARE AN IRRESISTIBLE COMBINATION. FOR A SPECIAL TOUCH GRATE THE WHITE CHOCOLATE OVER THE RISOTTO, JUST BEFORE SERVING TO PREVENT IT MELTING TOTALLY.

1 l (1¾ pts) milk
50 g (2 oz) butter
400 g (14 oz) arborio rice
4 Tbsp orange liqueur
150 ml (¼ pt) orange juice
50 g (2 oz) milk chocolate, grated

2 oranges, peeled and cut into segments
25 g (1 oz) white chocolate, coarsely grated to garnish

1 Pour the milk into a saucepan and bring to the boil. Reduce the heat to a gentle simmer.

2 Meanwhile, melt the butter in a pan and gently cook the rice for 2 minutes, stirring, until the rice is well-coated in butter. Stir in the orange liqueur and orange juice and cook gently, stirring, until absorbed.

3 Add a ladleful of milk to the rice and cook, stirring, until absorbed. Continue adding small quantities of milk for a further 20 minutes. Stir in the milk chocolate and orange sections. Continue to cook for a further 5 minutes until the risotto is thick but not sticky. Sprinkle the white chocolate over the top, and serve.

tiramisù risotto

THIS IS A TRADITIONAL, RICH DESSERT ASSOCIATED WITH, AND LOVED BY, ITALIANS.

950 ml (1 ½ pts) milk

300 ml (½ pt) double cream

50 g (2 oz) butter

400 g (14 oz) arborio rice

4 Tbsp strong black coffee

1 Tbsp cocoa powder

2 Tbsp caster sugar

3 Tbsp brandy

50 g (2 oz) coarsely grated plain chocolate

1 Pour the milk and cream into a saucepan and bring to the boil. Reduce the heat to a gentle simmer.

2 Meanwhile, melt the butter in a large frying pan and stir in the rice. Cook gently, stirring, for 2 minutes until the rice is well-coated in butter. Mix the coffee, cocoa, sugar and brandy together and stir into the rice with a ladleful of milk and cream mixture.

3 Cook gently, stirring, until absorbed. Continue adding the cream and milk in small quantities for a further 25 minutes. Stir in the chocolate and serve in a warm dish.

cream cheese & apricot risotto

CHEESE AND APRICOTS TASTE GOOD TOGETHER WHEN LIGHTLY SWEETENED. USE FULL-FAT CREAM CHEESE IF POSSIBLE AND RIPE APRICOTS FOR BETTER FLAVOUR.

1.25 l (2 pts) apricot juice

50 g (2 oz) butter

2 tsp ground allspice

400 g (14 oz) arborio rice

225 g (8 oz) cream cheese

2 Tbsp icing sugar, sifted

350 g (12 oz) fresh apricots, stoned and quartered

Lemon balm, to garnish

1 Pour the apricot juice into a saucepan and bring to the boil. Reduce the heat to a gentle simmer.

2 Meanwhile, melt the butter in a large frying pan and gently cook the allspice and rice for 2 minutes, stirring, until the rice is well-coated in butter.

3 Add a ladleful of apricot juice and cook gently, stirring, until absorbed. Continue adding small quantities of juice to the rice until half has been used. Stir in the cream cheese and sugar.

4 Continue adding the juice until the risotto is thick but not sticky, about 25 minutes. Stir in the apricots and cook for a further 5 minutes. Serve garnished with lemon balm.

OPPOSITE TIRAMISÙ RISOTTO

raspberry, peach & hazelnut risotto

THIS COLOURFUL COMBINATION OF INGREDIENTS IS USUALLY FOUND IN THE CLASSIC DESSERT PEACH MELBA. STIRRED INTO RICE SWEETENED WITH PEACH NECTAR, IT IS SENSATIONAL.

625 ml (1 pt) milk

300 ml (½ pt) double cream

300 ml (½ pt) peach nectar

50 g (2 oz) butter

50 g (2 oz) coarsely chopped hazelnuts

400 g (14 oz) arborio rice

2 Tbsp icing sugar

225 g (8 oz) tinned or fresh peach quarters

65 g (2½ oz) raspberries

Sprigs mint, to decorate

1 Pour the milk and cream into a saucepan with the peach nectar and bring to the boil. Reduce the heat to a gentle simmer.

2 Meanwhile, melt the butter in a large frying pan and gently cook the nuts for 1 minute, stirring. Add the rice and cook, stirring, for a further 2 minutes until the rice is well-coated in butter.

3 Add a ladleful of the milk, cream and nectar mixture and cook gently, stirring, until absorbed. Stir in the sugar and continue adding the liquid in small quantities for a further 20 minutes.

4 Gently stir in the peaches and raspberries, cook for 4 to 5 minutes until the risotto is thick but not sticky. Serve in a warm dish, decorated with mint.

summer fruits risotto

NOTHING QUITE BEATS THE FLAVOURS OF MIXED SUMMER FRUITS. STIR THEM VERY GENTLY INTO THE RISOTTO SO THAT THEY DO NOT BREAK UP.

950 ml (1½ pts) milk

300 ml (½ pt) double cream

50 g (2 oz) butter

400 g (14 oz) arborio rice

1 tsp ground cinnamon

2 Tbsp caster sugar

2 Tbsp kirsch

450 g (1 lb) mixed summer fruits such as strawberries, raspberries, blueberries, red- and blackcurrants

1 Tbsp chopped fresh mint

1 Pour the milk and cream into a saucepan and bring to the boil. Immediately reduce the heat to a gentle simmer, and keep simmering.

2 Meanwhile, melt the butter in a large frying pan and gently cook the rice in it, stirring, until well-coated in the butter.

3 Add a ladleful of the milk and cream mixture and cook gently, stirring, until absorbed. Add the cinnamon, sugar and kirsch and continue adding small quantities of milk and cream until the risotto is thick but not sticky. Gently stir in the fruit and mint and serve.

OPPOSITE SUMMER FRUITS RISOTTO

lemon & sultana risotto

THIS IS A TANGY DESSERT WITH FRESH LEMON JUICE AND ZEST, FLAVOURED WITH NUTMEG.

950 ml (1½ pts) milk

300 ml (½ pt) double cream

75 g (3 oz) butter

400 g (14 oz) arborio rice

Juice and zest of 1 lemon

1 tsp freshly grated nutmeg

2 Tbsp light brown sugar

50 g (2 oz) sultanas

1 lemon, halved and sliced

1 Pour the milk and cream into a saucepan and bring to the boil. Reduce the heat to a gentle simmer.

2 Meanwhile, melt 50 grams (2 ounces) of the butter in a large frying pan and cook the rice for 2 minutes, stirring, until the rice is well-coated.

3 Add a ladleful of the milk and cream mixture with the lemon juice and zest and cook gently, stirring, until the liquid is absorbed. Stir in the nutmeg and sugar, and continue adding small quantities of milk and cream for a further 20 minutes.

4 Stir in the sultanas and continue cooking for a further 5 minutes until the risotto is thick but not sticky. Meanwhile, melt the remaining butter in a separate frying pan and cook the lemon slices for 2 to 3 minutes, turning: Stir the contents of the pan into the risotto and serve in a warm dish.

sunshine fruit risotto

THIS IS A REALLY COLOURFUL RECIPE IN BOTH PRESENTATION AND FLAVOUR. CHOOSE FRUITS AT THEIR PRIME.

1.25 l (2 pts) pineapple juice

50 g (2 oz) butter

2 Tbsp soft brown sugar

400 g (14 oz) arborio rice

1 tsp ground cinnamon

1 tsp ground allspice

225 g (8 oz) fresh pineapple, peeled, cored and cubed

2 bananas, peeled and sliced

1 papaya, halved, seeded and sliced

1 mango, peeled and sliced

1 Pour the pineapple juice into a saucepan and bring to the boil. Reduce the heat to a gentle simmer.

2 Meanwhile, melt the butter in a large frying pan and stir in the sugar and rice. Add the spices and cook gently, stirring, until the rice is well-coated in butter.

3 Add a ladleful of pineapple juice and cook gently, stirring, until absorbed. Continue adding pineapple juice in small quantities for 20 minutes. Stir in the fruit and cook for a further 5 minutes until the risotto is thick but not sticky. Serve in a warm dish.

apple, pear & cinnamon risotto

THIS IS A REAL ORCHARD DESSERT, DELICATELY FLAVOURED
WITH CINNAMON TO BRING OUT THE BEST IN THE FRUITS.

1.25 l (2 pts) apple juice

50 g (2 oz) butter

2 tsp ground cinnamon

2 Tbsp soft brown sugar

400 g (14 oz) arborio rice

2 red dessert apples, cored and sliced

2 dessert pears, cored and sliced

25 g (1 oz) pecan halves

1 Pour the apple juice into a saucepan and bring to the boil. Reduce the heat to a gentle simmer.

2 Meanwhile, melt half of the butter in a large frying pan and add the cinnamon, sugar and rice. Cook gently, stirring, for 2 minutes until the rice is coated.

3 Add a ladleful of apple juice and gently cook, stirring, until absorbed. Continue adding apple juice in small quantities until the risotto is thick but not sticky, about 25 minutes.

4 Meanwhile, melt the remaining butter in a separate frying pan and cook the apples, pears and pecans for 3 to 4 minutes, stirring. Add the fruit and pecans to the rice, mix gently and serve.

Index